pancakes,
crêpes, waffles
& french toast

pancakes, crêpes, waffles & french toast

irresistible recipes from the griddle

Hannah Miles

photography by Steve Painter

RYLAND PETERS & SMALL

LONDON • NEW YORK

Dedication

For my dear friend Maren, with fond memories of Canadian pancakes!

Design, photography and prop styling
Steve Painter
Commissioning Editor Stephanie Milner
Head of Production Patricia Harrington
Art Director Leslie Harrington
Editorial Director Julia Charles
Food Stylist Lucy McKelvie
Assistant Food Stylist Ellie Jarvis
Indexer Hilary Bird

First published in 2014 by
Ryland Peters & Small
20–21 Jockey's Fields London WC1R 4BW
and
519 Broadway, 5th Floor, New York
NY 10012
www.rylandpeters.com

Text © Hannah Miles 2014
Design and photographs © Ryland Peters
& Small 2014
Hand-stitched page backrounds made
by Bridget Rolfe

10 9 8 7 6 5 4 3 2 1

Printed in China

ISBN: 978-1-84975-487-3

A CIP record for this book is available from the British Library.

US Library of Congress CIP data has been applied for.

Notes

• All spoon measurements are level unless otherwise specified.
• All eggs are medium (UK) or large (US), unless otherwise specified. Uncooked or partially cooked eggs should not be served to the very old, frail, young children, pregnant women or those with compromised immune systems.
• When a recipe calls for the grated zest of citrus fruit, buy unwaxed fruit and wash well before using. If you can only find treated fruit, scrub well in warm soapy water before using.
• Ovens should be preheated to the specified temperatures. We recommend using an oven thermometer. If using a fan-assisted oven, adjust temperatures according to the manufacturer's instructions.

contents

Introduction

For almost as long as I can remember I have loved making pancakes and waffles. Pancakes were one of the first things I learnt to cook and I used to make them when I came home from school with hot golden syrup sauce. There are few things nicer to serve than waffles and pancakes for a relaxed weekend breakfast or brunch party. The best thing about pancakes, waffles and French toasts are that they are great standby recipes — needing only flour, milk, eggs and a little sugar (or bread for French toast). Pancakes, waffles and French toasts are not just for breakfast, they also make great lunch or supper dishes when you are in need of a quick and tasty meal. With a little maple syrup or simply lemon and sugar, these recipes can make a delicious treat in absolutely no time at all.

PANCAKES AND CRÊPES

Pancakes are served all around the world and have been documented in recipe books for centuries. There are two main types of pancake – crêpes, which are traditional French pancakes, made with a runny batter spread out very thinly in a pan or on a griddle, and American pancakes (or griddle cakes), which are made with a thick batter that includes raising agents so the resulting pancakes are light and fluffy. Both types are delicious and whatever your pancake preference, there is a recipe for you in the chapters of this book.

Crêpes can be rolled up around fillings (both sweet and savoury), such as the apple or tropical crêpes on pages 49 and 50 or the savoury varieties, stuffed with creamy chicken or spinach and ricotta, on pages 122 and 125. When it comes to American pancakes, not only are these thick pancakes delicious with lashings of sauce poured over, they can also have fillings within them, such as the blackberry pancakes on page 17, which contain a cream cheese and berry filling that is

hidden until you cut into the pancake, or the Baklava version on page 29 filled with honey and nuts.

Traditionally, pancakes and crêpes should be tossed in the pan to turn them over once the underside is cooked. In Olney, a market town near to where I live, there has been a pancake race on Shrove Tuesday since 1445 – in memory of a woman who was late for Church and ran there with a pancake pan in her hand, tossing it all the way. It is a great spectacle to watch, followed by a delicious pancake lunch. If you are not brave enough to toss your pancakes at home, simply flip them over with a spatula instead. It won't make any difference to the taste!

Crêpes and pancakes can both be made in a large frying pan/skillet, although to make the perfect crêpe you really need a crêpe pan or a crêpe machine, which is similar to a hot plate. If you want to make crêpes regularly, it is really worth investing in a crêpe machine (they are not very expensive) as they make perfectly thin, lace-like crêpes, just like you would buy in a French market.

WAFFLES

Waffles are made with a thick batter, lightened with whisked egg whites. You need a waffle iron to make them. There are two main types of waffle iron – electric or stove-top – and both come in a wide variety of patterns: rectangular; circular; heart-shaped; or even waffle fingers. I find that electric waffle irons have better temperature control than stove-top waffle pans.

The thing I like most about waffles is that the little holes are great to hold fillings and syrups. Waffle batter can be flavoured with almost anything, transforming a simple batter into something very special. My personal favourites are the apricot and white chocolate waffles on page 66, or the S'mores waffles – chocolate waffles sandwiched together with toasted marshmallows and melted chocolate – on page 73. Both recipes are extremely indulgent but utterly delicious!

Waffles really need to be served straight away. You can stack and serve them once all the waffle batter is cooked but they can go a little soft so are best eaten when they are still crispy. Serve them one by one as soon as they are cooked for best results.

FRENCH TOAST

French toast, *pain perdu*, or 'eggy bread'; no matter what you call this simple treat, it is indisputably delicious. The German's call them *arme Ritter* or 'poor knights', as when knights fell on hard times and couldn't afford meat, they are said to have bought stale bread and made this delicious toast instead. While French toast is most commonly just egg-coated bread fried in butter, the recipes in this book take this humble treat one step further by making pockets in each slice for filling, such as the peanut butter and jelly or white chocolate macadamia and blueberry variations on pages 102 and 110. I can't recommend stuffed French toast enough so, if you haven't tried it before, this is a real treat!

QUANTITIES

The quantities of ingredients in the recipes in this book are guidelines only, as how many pancakes or waffles each batch of batter will make very much depends on the size of your pan or waffle iron. If you want to make only a few waffles or pancakes, simply halve the ingredients where necessary. With the crêpe mixtures, as it is impossible to divide one egg and one egg yolk, the best thing to do is to beat the egg, remove a spoonful and discard it before adding half the quantity to the batter.

HINTS AND TIPS

• Take care not to over grease your pan. I usually add butter or oil to the pan before I start and then carefully wipe it with a paper towel to remove any excess fat. I usually find that the first pancake or waffle I cook is never as good as the later ones, probably as there is less grease in the pan when you make the later ones. It is rarely necessary to add further butter to the pan after you have first greased it.

• Make sure that you leave the batter to rest for the specified time as this allows the gluten in the flour to relax and, if using baking powder, bubbles to start forming in the batter.

• The consistency of your batter needs to be just right, so that it spreads easily when you put it into your pan to cook. If it is too thick, simply add a little more milk. Crêpe batter can sometimes be too thin and, if this is the case, the crêpes can tear when you turn them over. If this happens just add a little more sifted flour to your batter mixture and whisk in well. Finding the right batter texture is something you have to do by feel and experience.

• When it comes to turning your pancakes over make sure that you don't turn them too quickly. The batter on the top of the pancake should be almost completely cooked before you flip.

• For best results, serve your pancakes, crêpes, waffles and French toast immediately.

pancakes

american pancakes with whipped maple butter

The classic American pancake is light and fluffy and served with lashings of maple syrup. Here, they are also served with whipped maple butter. Whipped butters are a delicious treat and can be made in many flavours. You need to serve them straight away rather than storing them in the refrigerator, otherwise the butter will set and loose its fluffy texture. Alternatively, serve these pancakes with crispy bacon in place of the maple butter, like the savoury beer and bacon pancakes on page 121 – the sweet and salty combination is delicious.

160 g/1¼ cups self-raising/rising flour, sifted

1 teaspoon baking powder

1 egg, separated

1 teaspoon vanilla extract/vanilla bean paste

60 g/scant ⅓ cup caster/granulated sugar

a pinch of salt

250 ml/1 cup milk

3 tablespoons melted butter, plus extra for frying

FOR THE MAPLE BUTTER

115 g/1 stick butter

60 ml/¼ cup maple syrup, plus extra to serve

60 g/½ cup icing/confectioners' sugar, sifted

a large frying pan/skillet or griddle

Makes 12

To make the pancake batter, put the flour, baking powder, egg yolk, vanilla extract/vanilla bean paste, caster/granulated sugar, salt and milk in a large mixing bowl and whisk together. Add in the melted butter and whisk again. The batter should have a smooth, dropping consistency.

In a separate bowl, whisk the egg white to stiff peaks. Gently fold the whisked egg white into the batter mixture using a spatula. Cover and put in the refrigerator to rest for 30 minutes.

For the maple butter, whisk together the butter, maple syrup and icing/confectioners' sugar using an electric whisk until light and creamy. This is best made shortly before serving.

When you are ready to serve, remove your batter mixture from the refrigerator and stir once. Put a little butter in a large frying pan/skillet set over medium heat. Allow the butter to melt and coat the base of the pan, then ladle small amounts of the rested batter into the pan, leaving a little space between each, or if you want to make larger pancakes you can fill the pan to make one at a time. Cook until the underside of each pancake is golden brown and a few bubbles start to appear on the top – this will take about 2–3 minutes. Turn the pancakes over using a spatula and cook on the other side until golden brown. Cook the remaining batter in the same way in batches until it is all used up, adding a little butter to the pan each time, if required.

Serve the pancakes in a stack with a little maple butter and a drizzle of maple syrup on top.

mini choc chip pancakes

These mini pancakes are similar to scotch pancakes. They are plain and simple but have a hidden layer of chocolate chips in the middle. You can use any chocolate chips that you like. Although you could serve these pancakes with chocolate sauce or maple syrup — I like them just on their own with a dusting of icing sugar.

160 g/1¼ cups self-raising/rising flour, sifted

1 teaspoon baking powder

1 egg, separated

1 teaspoon vanilla extract/vanilla bean paste

2 tablespoons caster/granulated sugar

a pinch of salt

250 ml/1 cup milk

3 tablespoons melted butter, plus extra for frying

100g/⅔ cup chocolate chips (white, milk/semi-sweet, dark/bittersweet, or a mixture of all)

icing/confectioners' sugar, for dusting

a large frying pan/skillet or griddle

Makes 12

To make the pancake batter, put the flour, baking powder, egg yolk, caster/granulated sugar, vanilla extract/vanilla bean paste, salt and milk in a large mixing bowl and whisk together. Add in the melted butter and whisk again. The batter should have a smooth, dropping consistency.

In a separate bowl, whisk the egg white to stiff peaks. Gently fold the whisked egg white into the batter mixture using a spatula. Cover and put in the refrigerator to rest for 30 minutes.

When you are ready to serve, remove your batter mixture from the refrigerator and stir once. Put a little butter in a large frying pan/skillet set over a medium heat. Allow the butter to melt and coat the base of the pan, then ladle small amounts of batter into the pan, leaving a little space between each, and sprinkle a few chocolate chips in the centre of each pancake. Carefully spoon over a little more batter to cover the chocolate chips. Cook until the underside of each pancake is golden brown and a few bubbles start to appear on the top – this will take about 2–3 minutes. Turn the pancakes over using a spatula and cook on the other side until golden brown.

Cook the remaining batter in the same way in batches until it is all used up, adding a little butter to the pan each time, if required.

Dust with icing/confectioners' sugar and serve warm or cold.

granola pancakes with salty honey sauce

These are one of my favourite breakfast pancakes. They have a crunchy, oaty top and are served with a delicious, buttery, honey sauce. You can also add raisins, sultanas, dried berries and cherries to the batter for an extra fruity tang.

160 g/1¼ cups self-raising/rising flour, sifted

1 teaspoon baking powder

1 egg, separated

1 tablespoon orange blossom honey

a pinch of salt

250 ml/1 cup milk

3 tablespoons melted butter, plus extra for frying

120–150 g/1½ cups granola

FOR THE SAUCE

60 g/4 tablespoons butter

3½ tablespoons clear honey

½ teaspoon salt

120 ml/½ cup double/heavy cream

a large frying pan/skillet or griddle

Makes 6

To make the pancake batter, put the flour, baking powder, egg yolk, honey, salt and milk in a large mixing bowl and whisk together. Add in the melted butter and whisk again. The batter should have a smooth, dropping consistency.

In a separate bowl, whisk the egg white to stiff peaks. Gently fold the whisked egg white into the batter mixture using a spatula. Cover and put in the refrigerator to rest for 30 minutes.

For the sauce, heat the butter and honey in a small saucepan or pot until the butter has melted. Then add the salt and whisk in the cream over the heat. Keep the pan on the heat but turn it down to low to keep the sauce warm until you are ready to serve.

When you are ready to serve, remove your batter mixture from the refrigerator and stir once. Put a little butter in a large frying pan/skillet set over a medium heat. Allow the butter to melt and coat the base of the pan, then ladle the batter into the pan and sprinkle a little granola on top of the pancake. Cook until the underside of the pancake is golden brown and a few bubbles start to appear on the top – this will take about 2–3 minutes. Turn the pancake over using a spatula and cook on the other side until golden brown. Keep the pancake warm while you cook the remaining batter, adding a little more butter to the pan each time if necessary.

Serve the pancakes with the warm honey sauce poured over the top.

blackberry cream cheese pancakes

These pancakes have a hidden pocket of blackberry and cream cheese filling, a yummy surprise when you cut into them! Served with a tangy blackberry sauce and whipped cream, they are an indulgent pancake dessert.

160 g/1¼ cups self-raising/
rising flour, sifted

1 teaspoon baking powder

1 egg, separated

2 tablespoons caster/granulated
sugar

a pinch of salt

250 ml/1 cup milk

3 tablespoons melted butter,
plus extra for frying

FOR THE SAUCE AND FILLING

300 g/2¼ cups blackberries

120 ml/½ cup water

100 g/½ cup caster/granulated
sugar

100 g/½ cup cream cheese

250 ml/1 cup double/heavy cream,
whipped to stiff peaks, to serve

a large frying pan/skillet or griddle

Makes 6

Begin by making the blackberry sauce and filling. Place the blackberries in a saucepan or pot with the water and sugar together over a medium heat, and simmer for about 5 minutes until the fruit is soft and the liquid is syrupy. Leave to cool.

In a separate bowl, whisk together the cream cheese and 2 tablespoons of the cooled blackberries (fruit and syrup) to make the filling.

To make the pancake batter, put the flour, baking powder, egg yolk, caster/granulated sugar, salt and milk in a large mixing bowl and whisk together. Add in the melted butter and whisk again. The batter should have a smooth, dropping consistency.

In a separate bowl, whisk the egg white to stiff peaks. Gently fold the whisked egg white into the batter mixture using a spatula. Cover and put in the refrigerator to rest for 30 minutes.

When you are ready to serve, remove your batter mixture from the refrigerator and stir once. Put a little butter in a large frying pan/skillet set over a medium heat. Allow the butter to melt and coat the base of the pan, then ladle the batter into the pan and tip to spread the batter out into a circle. Place a spoonful of the blackberry filling in the centre of the pancake and carefully spread it out, leaving a gap between the filling and the edge of the pancake. Cover the filling with a little more pancake batter so that it is completely hidden. Cook until the underside of the pancake is golden brown and a few bubbles start to appear on the top – this will take about 2–3 minutes. Then turn the pancakes over using a spatula and cook on the other side until golden brown. Keep the pancakes warm while you cook the remaining batter in the same way, adding a little butter to the pan each time, if required.

Serve the pancakes with the reserved blackberry sauce and whipped cream on the side.

wake-me-up coffee pancakes

These are the perfect breakfast pancakes, with a real caffeine kick to wake you up in the morning. The coffee syrup is made with cocoa nibs which are a real delicacy. Cocoa nibs are fermented, dried, roasted cocoa pods, usually ground with sugar to make chocolate. They are delicious and good for you as they don't contain sugar but still have an amazing chocolate taste. They are available from health food stores and some supermarkets, or online.

160 g/1¼ cups self-raising/
rising flour, sifted

1 teaspoon baking powder

1 egg, separated

1 tablespoon caster/granulated
sugar

a pinch of salt

250 ml/1 cup iced milk coffee

3 tablespoons melted butter,
plus extra for frying

150 g/1 cup mascarpone cheese

150 ml/⅔ cup crème fraîche

icing/confectioners' sugar,
to taste (optional)

cocoa powder, to dust

FOR THE SYRUP

100 ml/⅓ cup plus 1 tablespoon
espresso coffee

60 ml/¼ cup coffee liqueur

100 g/½ cup plus 1 tablespoon
caster/granulated sugar

1 teaspoon cocoa nibs or coffee
beans

a large frying pan/skillet or griddle

Makes 12

Begin by making the coffee syrup. Put all of the syrup ingredients in a saucepan or pot and simmer over a gentle heat for about 5 minutes until thick and gloopy. Set aside to allow the flavours to infuse and the syrup to cool.

To make the pancake batter, put the flour, baking powder, egg yolk, caster/granulated sugar, salt and iced coffee in a large mixing bowl and whisk together. Add in the melted butter and whisk again. The batter should have a smooth, dropping consistency.

In a separate bowl, whisk the egg white to stiff peaks. Gently fold the whisked egg white into the batter mixture using a spatula. Cover and put in the refrigerator to rest for 30 minutes.

When you are ready to serve, remove your batter mixture from the refrigerator and stir once. Put a little butter in a large frying pan/skillet set over a medium heat. Allow the butter to melt and coat the base of the pan, then ladle small amounts of the batter into the pan, leaving a little space between each. Cook until the batter is just set then turn over and cook for a further 2–3 minutes. Once cooked, keep the pancakes warm while you cook the remaining batter, adding a little butter to the pan each time, if required.

When you are ready to serve, place the mascarpone cheese and crème fraîche in a bowl, adding a little icing sugar to sweeten if you wish, and whisk together well.

Serve the pancakes in a stack with a dollop of the mascarpone cream on top and a drizzle of syrup. Dust with a little cocoa powder and enjoy!

buttermilk blueberry pancakes with blueberry lime sauce

Until I ate blueberries with the Murphy family in America, I really didn't understand what all the fuss was about. Blueberries have a wonderful, explosive taste when fresh and in season, although they are available year-round in supermarkets and online. I have added a little lime juice to the sauce to give these pancakes extra zing, although you can omit this if you have a good source of fresh, flavourful blueberries.

160 g/1¼ cups self-raising/rising flour, sifted

1 teaspoon baking powder

1 egg, separated

60 g/scant ⅓ cup caster/granulated sugar

a pinch of salt

200 ml/¾ cup milk

80 ml/5 tablespoons buttermilk

3 tablespoons melted butter, plus extra for frying

100 g/¾ cup fresh blueberries

FOR THE SAUCE

300 g/2¼ cups blueberries

freshly squeezed juice of 3 limes

100 g/½ cup caster/granulated sugar

90 ml/6 tablespoons water

300 ml/1¼ cups double/heavy cream, whipped to soft peaks, to serve

a large frying pan/skillet or griddle

Makes 12

Begin by making the sauce. Place the blueberries, lime juice and caster/granulated sugar in a saucepan or pot with the water and simmer over a gentle heat for about 5–10 minutes until the fruit is soft and the sauce is thick and syrupy.

To make the pancake batter, put the flour, baking powder, egg yolk, caster/granulated sugar, salt, milk and buttermilk in a large mixing bowl and whisk together. Add in the melted butter and whisk again. The batter should have a smooth, dropping consistency.

In a separate bowl, whisk the egg white to stiff peaks. Gently fold the whisked egg white into the batter mixture using a spatula. Cover and put in the refrigerator to rest for 30 minutes.

When you are ready to serve, remove your batter mixture from the refrigerator and stir once. Put a little butter in a large frying pan/skillet set over a medium heat. Allow the butter to melt and coat the base of the pan, then ladle small amounts of the batter into the pan, leaving a little space between each. Sprinkle a few blueberries over the top of the pancake and cook until the underside of each pancake is golden brown and a few bubbles start to appear on the top – this will take about 2–3 minutes. Turn the pancakes over using a spatula and cook on the other side until golden brown. Keep the pancakes warm while you cook the remaining batter in the same way, adding a little more butter to the pan each time, if required, and sprinkling each pancake with blueberries.

Serve the pancakes in a stack, drizzled with the blueberry sauce and a dollop of whipped cream.

banana maple chocolate chip pancakes with maple butter sauce and caramelized bananas

There are few more comforting foods than banana pancakes. These are extra-indulgent, flavoured with maple syrup and bursting with chocolate chips. Served with caramelized bananas and a maple butter sauce, they're great on a cold day to lift your spirits.

2 ripe bananas, peeled

freshly squeezed juice of ½ lemon

60 ml/4 tablespoons maple syrup

a pinch of salt

180 g/1⅓ cups self-raising/rising flour, sifted

1 teaspoon baking powder

1 egg, separated

250 ml/1 cup plus 1 tablespoon milk

3 tablespoons melted butter, plus extra for frying

100g/⅔ cup milk/semi-sweet chocolate chips

FOR THE SAUCE

50 g/3½ tablespoons butter

80 ml/5 tablespoons maple syrup

120 ml/½ cup double/heavy cream

FOR THE CARAMELIZED BANANAS

4 ripe bananas, peeled and sliced

2 tablespoons caster/granulated sugar

a large frying pan/skillet or griddle

Makes 12

Begin by making the maple butter sauce. Heat the butter and maple syrup in a saucepan or pot set over a medium heat for 2–3 minutes, until the butter has melted. Add the cream to the pan and simmer over a gentle heat for a few minutes longer. If you want to serve the sauce warm, keep the pan on the heat but turn it down to low until you are ready to serve.

For the caramelized bananas, sprinkle the prepared slices with caster/granulated sugar, ensuring they are well coated. Set a frying pan/skillet over a high heat and place the sugar coated bananas into the pan without any butter or oil. Cook for a few minutes until the bananas start to caramelize, then turn the slices over and cook on the other side until golden brown. Remove the pan from the heat and set aside.

For the pancake batter, crush the 2 bananas to a smooth purée together with the lemon juice, using the back of a fork or in a food processor. Put the banana purée into a large mixing bowl and add the maple syrup, salt, flour, baking powder and egg yolk. Whisk the ingredients together, gradually adding the milk until the batter is smooth. Add the melted butter and whisk in. The batter should have a smooth dropping consistency.

In a separate bowl, whisk the egg white to stiff peaks. Gently fold the whisked egg white into the batter mixture together with the chocolate chips using a spatula. Cover and put in the refrigerator to rest for 30 minutes.

When you are ready to serve, remove your batter mixture from the refrigerator and stir once. Put a little butter in a large frying pan/skillet set over a medium heat. Allow the butter to melt and coat the base of the pan, then ladle small amounts of the batter into the pan, leaving a little space between each. Cook until the underside of each pancake is golden brown and a few bubbles start to appear on the top – this will take about 2–3 minutes. Turn the pancakes over using a spatula and cook on the other side until golden brown. Keep the pancakes warm while you cook the remaining batter, adding a little butter to the pan each time, if required.

To serve, top the pancakes with the caramelized bananas and drizzle with the maple butter sauce and any extra caramel from the pan.

fig and ricotta pancakes with orange syrup

Figs are one of those fruits that always remind me of summer. They are delicious in this recipe with their vibrant pink and green colour, served drizzled with buttery orange syrup in rich pancakes laden with ricotta. I make them small enough to top with just one fig slice, but you can make larger versions with several fig slices on top if you prefer.

160 g/1¼ cups self-raising/
rising flour, sifted

1 teaspoon baking powder

2 eggs, separated

the grated zest of 2 unwaxed
oranges

50 g/¼ cup caster/
granulated sugar

a pinch of salt

250 ml/1 cup milk

125 g/½ cup ricotta cheese

3 tablespoons melted butter,
plus extra for frying

4–5 ripe figs, thinly sliced

sugar nibs/pearl sugar or
caster/granulated sugar,
for sprinkling

FOR THE SYRUP

freshly squeezed juice of 4 oranges

100 g/½ cup caster/granulated
sugar

50 g/3½ tablespoons butter

a large frying pan/skillet or griddle

Makes 18

Begin by preparing the syrup. Put the orange juice, sugar and butter in a saucepan or pot over a medium heat and simmer until the sugar is melted. Keep the pan on the heat but turn it down to low to keep the syrup warm until you are ready to serve.

To make the pancake batter, put the flour, baking powder, egg yolks, orange zest, caster/granulated sugar, salt, milk and ricotta cheese in a large mixing bowl and whisk together. Add in the melted butter and whisk again. The batter should have a smooth, dropping consistency.

In a separate bowl, whisk the egg whites to stiff peaks. Gently fold the whisked egg whites into the batter mixture using a spatula. Cover and put in the refrigerator to rest for 30 minutes.

When you are ready to serve, remove your batter mixture from the refrigerator and stir once. Put a little butter in a large frying pan/skillet set over a medium heat. Allow the butter to melt and coat the base of the pan, then ladle small spoonfuls of batter into the pan, leaving a little space between each. Place a slice of fig on top of each pancake and sprinkle with sugar nibs/pearl sugar or caster/granulated sugar. Cook until the underside of each pancake is golden brown and a few bubbles start to appear on the top – this will take about 1–2 minutes. Turn the pancakes over using a spatula and cook on the other side until the sugar-topped figs have caramelized and the top is golden brown. Keep the pancakes warm while you cook the remaining batter until it is used up.

Serve the pancakes immediately with a drizzle of the orange syrup.

chai pancakes with rose petals

I love chai tea, with its delicate hint of cardamom, and use it to infuse the milk to make the pancake batter for this recipe. Served with a delicate rose cream and twinkling with a little gold leaf, these are special occasion pancakes.

375 ml/1½ cups milk

1 chai teabag

½ cinnamon stick

a pinch of saffron

8 cardamom pods

2 tablespoons caster/granulated sugar

160 g/1¼ cups self-raising/rising flour, sifted

2 teaspoons baking powder

a pinch of salt

1 egg

3 tablespoons melted butter, plus extra for frying

a handful of chopped pistachios, to serve

edible gold leaf, to serve (optional)

pink pearl sugar/sugar nibs, to serve (optional)

FOR THE CRYSTALLIZED ROSE PETALS

1 egg white

1 pesticide-free rose, petals removed

caster/granulated sugar

FOR THE CREAM

200 ml/¾ cup double/heavy cream

1 tablespoon rose syrup, plus extra to serve

1 tablespoon icing/confectioners' sugar

a silicon mat or baking sheet lined with baking parchment

a large frying pan/skillet or griddle

Makes 8

Prepare the crystallized rose petals a day in advance. Take care to only use roses that have not been sprayed with any chemicals or pesticides. Whisk the egg white until it forms a foam. Paint a thin layer of the whisked egg white on both the front and the back of each petal and sprinkle it with caster/granulated sugar. This is best achieved by holding the sugar at a small height above the petal and sprinkling lightly – place a plate or tray beneath the petal to catch any excess sugar. It is important to ensure that all the egg white is coated in sugar, so it is best to work on one petal at a time. Repeat with all the remaining petals and place them on the prepared silicon mat or baking sheet. Transfer the petals to a warm place to dry overnight. Once dried, store the crystallized petals in an airtight container for up to 3 weeks until you are ready to serve.

To make the pancake batter, heat the milk in a saucepan or pot with the chai teabag, cinnamon, saffron, cardamom pods and caster/granulated sugar. Bring to the boil, then remove from the heat. Take out the teabag and discard. Leave the remaining spices in the milk to infuse and set aside to cool.

Once the spiced milk has cooled, remove the cinnamon and cardamom pods using a spoon and discard. Then put the flour, baking powder, salt, egg and spiced milk in a large mixing bowl and whisk together. Add the melted butter and whisk again. The batter should have a smooth dropping consistency. Cover and put in the refrigerator to rest for 30 minutes.

For the rose cream, put all of the ingredients into a mixing bowl and whisk to stiff peaks. Cover and store in the refrigerator until needed.

When you are ready to serve, remove your batter mixture from the refrigerator and stir once. Put a little butter in a large frying pan/skillet set over a medium heat. Allow the butter to melt and coat the base of the pan, then ladle small amounts of the batter into the pan, leaving a little space between each. Cook until the underside of each pancake is golden brown and a few bubbles start to appear on the top – this will take about 2–3 minutes. Turn the pancakes over using a spatula and cook on the other ide until golden brown. Keep the pancakes warm while you cook the remaining batter, adding a little butter to the pan each time, if required.

Top the pancakes with a generous spoonful of rose cream and sprinkle with the pistachios, crystallized rose petals, gold leaf and pink pearl sugar/sugar nibs. Drizzle with a little rose syrup and serve.

baklava pancakes

Greek baklava was one of the first desserts I learnt to make — utterly delicious with candied cinnamon and walnuts, layered between buttery filo pastry. I have taken inspiration from the baklava filling for these pancakes, by including a hidden pocket of walnut butter. Serve drizzled with Greek honey.

160 g/1¼ cups self-raising/rising flour, sifted

1 teaspoon baking powder

1 egg

50 g/¼ cup caster/granulated sugar

120 ml/½ cup milk

280 ml/1¼ cups buttermilk

3 tablespoons melted butter, plus extra for frying

½ teaspoon salt

Greek runny honey, to serve

FOR THE FILLING

100 g/1 cup chopped walnuts

2 teaspoons ground cinnamon

50 g/¼ cup caster/granulated sugar

90 g/6 tablespoons butter, softened

a large frying pan/skillet or griddle

Makes 6

To make the pancake batter, put the flour, baking powder, egg, caster/granulated sugar, salt, milk and buttermilk in a large mixing bowl and whisk together. Add in the melted butter and whisk again. The batter should have a smooth, pourable consistency. Cover and put in the refrigerator to rest for 30 minutes.

For the baklava filling, blitz the walnuts to a fine crumb with the cinnamon and sugar in a food processor. Transfer to a bowl then add the butter and mix together to a smooth paste. Set aside.

When you are ready to serve, remove the batter mixture from the refrigerator and stir once. Put a little butter in a large frying pan/skillet set over a medium heat. Allow the butter to melt and coat the base of the pan, then ladle small amounts of the batter into the pan. Put a spoonful of the baklava filling in the centre of the pancake and carefully spread it out, leaving a gap between the filling and the edge of the pancake. Cover the filling with a little more pancake batter so that it is completely hidden. Cook until the underside of each pancake is golden brown and a few bubbles start to appear on the top – this will take about 2–3 minutes. Turn the pancake over using a spatula and cook on the other side until golden brown. Keep the pancakes warm while you cook the remaining batter, adding a little butter to the pan each time, if required.

Serve the pancakes warm with a drizzle of honey over the top.

oreo pancakes with chocolate fudge sauce

I ate these pancakes at a fantastic diner in New York and was instantly hooked. The Oreo pieces soften when cooked and create delicious chocolate bursts within the pancake. Served with a wickedly sweet chocolate sauce, these are definitely pancakes for a special treat rather than every day.

160 g/1¼ cups self-raising/rising flour, sifted

1 teaspoon baking powder

1 egg, separated

1 teaspoon vanilla extract/vanilla bean paste

2 tablespoons caster/granulated sugar

a pinch of salt

250 ml/1 cup milk

2 tablespoons melted butter, plus extra for frying

9 Oreo cookies or similar, broken into pieces

FOR THE SAUCE

30 g/⅓ cup cocoa powder, sifted

1 teaspoon cold water

150 ml/⅔ cup double/heavy cream

100 g/⅓ cup milk/semi-sweet chocolate, chopped

1 tablespoon golden syrup/light corn syrup

1 tablespoon butter

a pinch of salt

1 teaspoon vanilla extract/vanilla bean paste

a large frying pan/skillet or griddle

Makes 12

To make the pancake batter, put the flour, baking powder, egg yolk, vanilla extract/vanilla bean paste, caster/granulated sugar, salt and milk in a large mixing bowl and whisk together. Add in the melted butter and whisk again. The batter should have a smooth, dropping consistency.

In a separate bowl, whisk the egg white to stiff peaks. Gently fold the whisked egg white into the batter mixture using a spatula. Cover and put in the refrigerator to rest for 30 minutes.

For the chocolate fudge sauce, mix the cocoa powder with a little cold water until you have smooth paste. Put the cream, chocolate, cocoa paste, golden syrup/light corn syrup, butter, salt and vanilla extract in a saucepan or pot set over a medium heat and simmer until the chocolate has melted and you have a smooth, glossy sauce. Keep the pan on the heat but turn it down to low to keep the sauce warm until you are ready to serve.

When you are ready to serve, remove your batter mixture from the refrigerator and stir once. Put a little butter in a large frying pan/skillet set over a medium heat. Allow the butter to melt and coat the base of the pan, then ladle small amounts of the batter into the pan. Sprinkle some of the Oreo cookies into the batter and cook until the batter is just set then turn over and cook for a further 2–3 minutes. Once cooked, keep the pancakes warm while you cook the remaining batter in the same way, adding a little butter to the pan each time, if required.

Serve the pancakes in a stack with the hot chocolate fudge sauce poured over the top.

coconut chocolate pancakes

Coconut and chocolate make a great pancake combination. With a crunch of toasted, shredded coconut and coconut syrup, these pancakes are a coconut-lover's dream. If you cannot find long shredded soft coconut, substitute desiccated coconut instead.

160 g/1¼ cups self-raising/rising flour, sifted

1 teaspoon baking powder

1 egg, separated

1 teaspoon vanilla extract/vanilla bean paste

60 g/scant ⅓ cup caster/granulated sugar

a pinch of salt

250 ml/1 cup milk

3 tablespoons melted butter, plus extra for frying

100 g/⅔ cup plain/bittersweet or milk/semi-sweet chocolate chips

150 g/2 cups long shredded soft coconut

FOR THE SAUCE

200 ml/¾ cup coconut milk

75 g/⅓ cup caster/granulated sugar

a large frying pan/skillet or griddle

Makes 6

To make the pancake batter, put the flour, baking powder, egg yolk, caster/granulated sugar, salt and milk in a large mixing bowl and whisk together. Add in the melted butter and whisk again. The batter should have a smooth, dropping consistency.

In a separate bowl, whisk the egg white to stiff peaks. Gently fold the whisked egg white, the chocolate chips and half of the shredded coconut into the batter mixture using a spatula. Cover and put in the refrigerator to rest for 30 minutes.

Toast the remaining coconut in a dry frying pan until lightly golden brown. Take care to watch it closely as it can burn easily.

For the sauce, put the coconut milk and sugar in a saucepan or pot set over a medium heat and simmer for about 5 minutes until the mixture turns syrupy. Keep the pan on the heat but turn it down to low to keep the sauce warm until you are ready to serve.

When you are ready to serve, remove your batter mixture from the refrigerator and stir gently. Put a little butter in a large frying pan/skillet set over a medium heat. Allow the butter to melt and coat the base of the pan, then ladle a little of the batter into the pan. Sprinkle a tablespoon of toasted coconut over the top of the pancake and cook until the underside is golden brown and a few bubbles start to appear on the top – this will take about 2–3 minutes. Turn the pancake over using a spatula and cook on the other side until golden brown. Keep the pancakes warm while you cook the remaining batter in the same way, adding a little more butter to the pan each time if required.

Serve the pancakes warm sprinkled with the remaining toasted coconut and a drizzle of coconut sauce.

oatmeal pancakes with berry compote

These are great breakfast pancakes — with oatmeal soaked in milk mixed into the batter and candied oats on top. Served with a warm berry compote and crème fraîche, they are the perfect pancakes to make in the summer, when you have a glut of fresh berries to use up.

370–400 ml/1½ cups milk

200 g/1½ cups self-raising/rising flour, sifted

2 teaspoon baking powder

1 egg

a pinch of salt

1 tablespoon caster/granulated sugar

3 tablespoons melted butter, plus extra for frying

crème fraîche, to serve (optional)

FOR THE COMPOTE

500 g/4 cups summer berries (raspberries, blueberries, strawberries and blackberries in any combination of your choosing), stalks removed

250 ml/1 cup water

100 g/½ cup caster/granulated sugar

1 teaspoon vanilla extract/vanilla bean paste

freshly squeezed juice of 1 lemon

FOR THE TOASTED OATS

60 g/½ cup oatmeal

50 g/¼ tablespoon caster/granulated sugar

a large frying pan/skillet or griddle

Makes 10

Begin by preparing the compote. Put the summer berries in a saucepan or pot set over a medium heat with the water, sugar, vanilla extract/vanilla bean paste and lemon juice. Simmer until the sugar has dissolved and the fruit is just starting to soften but still holds its shape. This will take about 5 minutes. Set aside to cool then store in the refrigerator until you are ready to serve.

For the toasted oats, place the oats and sugar in a dry frying pan/ skillet set over a medium heat and toast for a few minutes until the sugar starts to caramelize the oats. Remove from the heat and set aside to cool.

Soak half of the toasted oats in 250 ml/1 cup of the milk for about 30 minutes, until plump. Reserving the rest of the oats for the pancake batter.

To make the pancake batter, put the flour, baking powder, egg, salt, caster/granulated sugar and milk-soaked oats in a large mixing bowl and whisk together. Add in the melted butter and whisk again. Gradually add the remaining milk until you have a smooth, pourable batter. Be careful not to make the batter too thin when adding the remaining milk – you may not need it all. Cover and put in the refrigerator to rest for 30 minutes.

When you are ready to serve, remove your batter mixture from the refrigerator and stir once. Put a little butter in a large frying pan/skillet set over a medium heat. Allow the butter to melt and coat the base of the pan, then ladle small amounts of the batter into the pan. Sprinkle some of the reserved toasted oats over the top of the pancake and cook until the underside is golden brown and a few bubbles start to appear on the top – this will take about 2–3 minutes. Turn the pancake over using a spatula and cook on the other side until golden brown. Keep the pancakes warm while you cook the remaining batterin the same way, adding a little more butter to the pan each time if required.

Serve the pancakes with the cooled berry compote and crème fraîche.

crêpes

crêpes with lemon and sugar

Although these are the simplest of pancakes, they will always remain my favourite. So simple, with just a squeeze of lemon and a sprinkling of sugar, but they taste divine. You can replace the lemon juice with a squeeze of lime or orange juice for equally tangy results.

140 g/1 cup plain/all-purpose flour, sifted

1 egg and 1 egg yolk

2 tablespoons melted butter, cooled, plus extra for frying

15 g/1 heaped tablespoon caster/granulated sugar

a pinch of salt

300 ml/1¼ cups milk

a sprinkling of caster/granulated sugar, to serve

2 lemons, cut into wedges, to serve

a large frying pan/skillet, griddle or crêpe pan/machine

a crêpe swizzle stick (optional)

Makes 10

To make the crêpe batter, put the flour, egg and egg yolk, melted butter, caster/granulated sugar and salt in a large mixing bowl. Whisking all the time, gradually add the milk until you have a smooth and runny batter. Cover and put the batter in the refrigerator to rest for 30 minutes.

When you are ready to serve, remove the batter from the refrigerator and stir gently. Put a little butter in a large frying pan/skillet set over medium heat. Allow the butter to melt and coat the base of the pan, then ladle a small amount of the rested batter into the pan and quickly spread it out very thinly. You can do this either by tilting the pan, or, for best results, use a crêpe swizzle stick. Cook until the top of the pancake is set then turn over carefully with a spatula and cook on the other side for a further 1–2 minutes until the crêpe is golden brown. Keep the crêpes warm while you cook the remaining batter in the same way.

Serve sprinkled with sugar, with lemon wedges on the side to squeeze the juice over the top, as desired.

raspberry crêpes

Raspberries are my favourite summer fruit — I love their tangy taste. My mum grows them in abundance on her allotment and I love to pick them for tarts, pavlovas and these delicious crêpes. Freeze-dried raspberry pieces are available in most good supermarkets or online, for when the fresh raspberry season has passed.

140 g/1 cup plain/all-purpose flour, sifted

1 egg and 1 egg yolk

2 tablespoons melted butter, cooled, plus extra for frying

15 g/1 heaped tablespoon caster/granulated sugar

a pinch of salt

300 ml/1¼ cups milk

FOR THE SYRUP AND FILLING

800 g/5½ cups fresh raspberries

2 tablespoons icing/confectioners' sugar, sifted

250 ml/1 cup double/heavy cream, whipped to stiff peaks

a handful of freeze-dried raspberry pieces

a large frying pan/skillet, griddle or crêpe pan/machine

a crêpe swizzle stick (optional)

Makes 10

Begin by making a raspberry syrup. Press half of the fresh raspberries through a fine meshed sieve/strainer set over a mixing bowl, to release the juice and remove the seeds. Discard the seeds. Add the icing/confectioners' sugar to the raspberry juice and whisk together.

To make the crêpe batter, put the flour, egg and egg yolk, melted butter, caster/granulated sugar and salt in a large mixing bowl. Whisking all the time, gradually add the milk until you have a smooth and runny batter. Add 1 tablespoon of the raspberry syrup and whisk again. Cover and put the batter in the refrigerator to rest for 30 minutes.

While the batter is resting, fold half of the raspberry syrup into the whipped cream so that ripples of syrup run through it. Set aside in the refrigerator until needed.

When you are ready to serve, remove the batter from the refrigerator and stir gently. Put a little butter in a large frying pan/skillet set over medium heat. Allow the butter to melt and coat the base of the pan, then ladle a small amount of the rested batter into the pan and quickly spread the batter out very thinly. You can do this either by tilting the pan, or, for best results, use a crêpe swizzle stick. Cook until the top of the pancake is set then turn over carefully with a spatula and cook on the other side for a further 1–2 minutes until the crêpe is golden brown. Keep the crêpes warm while you cook the remaining batter in the same way.

Spoon the raspberry syrup and filling onto one half of each crêpe, then top with a handful of the reserved whole raspberries. Fold the crêpe in half and then half again.

Sprinkle with freeze-dried raspberries, drizzle with the remaining raspberry syrup and serve.

honey crêpes

There are few things nicer than eating a thick slice of bread spread with honey. As an alternative, why not try these delicate pancakes, fragranced with honey and topped with a honey sauce and honey crumble. I imagine that Winnie the Pooh (who loves honey as much as I do) would like these a lot!

160 g/1⅓ cups plain/all-purpose flour, sifted

1 egg and 1 egg yolk

2 tablespoons melted butter, cooled, plus extra for frying

1 tablespoon honey

300 ml/1¼ cups milk

FOR THE HONEY STREUSEL

90 g/⅔ cup plain/all-purpose flour, sifted

60 g/4 tablespoons butter

25 g/2 tablespoons caster/granulated sugar

1 scant tablespoon honey

FOR THE SAUCE

40 g/3 tablespoons butter

1 heaped tablespoon set honey

a pinch of salt or vanilla salt

250 ml/1 cup double/heavy cream

a large frying pan/skillet, griddle or crêpe pan/machine

a crêpe swizzle stick (optional)

a baking sheet, lined with baking parchment

Makes 10

Preheat the oven to 180°C (350°F) Gas 4.

For the honey streusel, rub the butter into the flour with your fingertips in a large mixing bowl. Add in the sugar and honey and continue rubbing together to make large crumbs. Sprinkle the crumbs loosely over the prepared baking sheet and bake in the preheated oven for 15–20 minutes until golden brown. Leave to cool, then break into small pieces. Store in an airtight container for up to 5 days until you are ready to serve.

To make the crêpe batter, put the flour, egg and egg yolk, melted butter, honey and salt in a large mixing bowl. Whisking all the time, gradually add the milk until you have a smooth and runny batter. Cover and put the batter in the refrigerator to rest for 30 minutes.

While the batter is resting, make the sauce. Heat the butter and honey in a saucepan or pot set over a medium heat until both are melted. Stir in the double/heavy cream and simmer for a few minutes longer. Keep the pan on the heat but turn it down to low to keep the sauce warm until you are ready to serve.

Remove the batter from the refrigerator and stir gently. Put a little butter in a large frying pan/skillet set over medium heat. Allow the butter to melt and coat the base of the pan, then ladle a small amount of the rested batter into the pan and quickly spread it out very thinly. You can do this either by tilting the pan, or, for best results, use a crêpe swizzle stick. Cook until the top of the pancake is set then turn over carefully with a spatula and cook on the other side for a further 1–2 minutes until the crêpe is golden brown. Keep the crêpes warm while you cook the remaining batter in the same way.

Serve the crêpes with the honey sauce on the side and the streusel sprinkled over the top.

chocolate hazelnut crêpes

These Nutella inspired crêpes are made with ground hazelnuts that give them a lovely texture. For best results, roast the hazelnuts yourself as this releases their oil and improves the flavour. If you are short of time you can buy ready-roasted hazelnuts in the supermarket.

140 g/1 cup plain/all-purpose flour, sifted

1 egg and 1 egg yolk

2 tablespoons melted butter, cooled, plus extra for frying

15 g/1 heaped tablespoon caster/granulated sugar

a pinch of salt

300 ml/1¼ cups milk

icing sugar/confectioners' sugar, to dust

FOR THE ROASTED HAZELNUTS

200 g/1½ cups whole hazelnuts

FOR THE SAUCE

100 g/¾ cups icing/confectioners' sugar, sifted

50 g/3½ tablespoons butter

120 ml/½ cup double/heavy cream

150 g/1 cup plain/bittersweet chocolate, chopped

a baking sheet lined with baking parchment

a sauce bottle fitted with a small, round nozzle/tip

a large frying pan/skillet, griddle or crêpe pan/machine

Makes 10

Begin by preparing the roasted hazelnuts. Preheat the oven to 180°C (350°F) Gas 4. Spread the nuts in a single layer on the prepared baking sheet and roast in the preheated oven for about 10 minutes until they are lightly golden brown and have just started to release their oil. Watch carefully towards the end of cooking to ensure that the nuts do not burn – they may need less cooking time if your oven is hot so remove them as soon as they start to turn golden brown. If the nuts have their skins on, rub them in a clean, dry cloth while still hot to remove them. Roughly chop a quarter of the nuts. Set aside until you are ready to serve. Pulse the remaining nuts to a fine crumb in a food processor.

To make the crêpe batter, put the flour, egg and egg yolk, melted butter, caster/granulated sugar and salt in a large mixing bowl. Whisking all the time, gradually add the milk until you have a smooth and runny batter. Fold in 50 g/½ cup of the fine hazelnut crumbs then cover and put the batter in the refrigerator to rest for 30 minutes.

While the batter is resting, make the hazelnut chocolate sauce. Put the icing/confectioners' sugar, butter, cream, chocolate and 100 g/1 cup of the fine hazelnut crumbs in a saucepan or pot set over a medium heat and simmer until the chocolate has melted and you have a smooth, glossy sauce. Keep the pan on the heat but turn it down to low to keep the sauce warm until you are ready to serve.

Remove the batter from the refrigerator and stir gently. Transfer the batter to the sauce bottle. Then put a little butter in a large frying pan/skillet set over medium heat. Allow the butter to melt and coat the base of the pan, then draw ornate heart shapes in the pan with the hazelnut batter. Cook until the batter on top of the crêpes is set then turn over very carefully with a spatula and cook on the other side for a further 1–2 minutes until the crêpe is golden brown. Keep the crêpes warm while you cook the remaining batter in the same way.

Serve immediately with the hot chocolate hazelnut sauce and extra roughly chopped hazelnuts over the top.

cherry jubilee

These Amaretto-flavoured crêpes are filled with lemon-scented cherries, whipped cream, ice cream and toasted almonds. They are a true retro diner classic — completely kitsch and over the top but so utterly delicious.

140 g/1 cup plain/all-purpose flour, sifted

1 egg and 1 egg yolk

2 tablespoons melted butter, cooled, plus extra for frying

15 g/1 heaped tablespoon caster/granulated sugar

1 tablespoon Amaretto or other almond liqueur

a pinch of salt

300 ml/1¼ cups milk

a handful of flaked/slivered almonds

8 scoops vanilla ice cream, to serve

FOR THE FILLING

400 g/1½ cups red cherry pie filling

250 g/1¼ cups fresh cherries, pitted

freshly squeezed juice of 1 lemon

FOR THE CREAM

300 ml/1¼ cups double/heavy cream

30 ml/2 tablespoons Amaretto or other almond liqueur

a large frying pan/skillet, griddle or crêpe pan/machine

a crêpe swizzle stick (optional)

a piping bag fitted with a large star nozzle

Makes 8

To make the crêpe batter, put the flour, egg and egg yolk, melted butter, caster/granulated sugar, Amaretto and salt in a large mixing bowl. Whisking all the time, gradually add the milk until you have a smooth and runny batter. Cover and put the batter in the refrigerator to rest for 30 minutes.

While the batter is resting, make the filling. Heat the cherry pie filling, pitted cherries and lemon juice in a saucepan or pot set over a medium heat until warmed through. Keep the pan on the heat but turn it down to low to keep the sauce warm until you are ready to serve.

Whip the cream to stiff peaks with the Amaretto in a separate mixing bowl and store in the refrigerator.

Toast the almonds in a dry frying pan/skillet set over a high heat until they are lightly golden brown, taking care that they do not burn. Remove from the pan and set aside.

When you are ready to serve, remove the batter from the refrigerator and stir gently. Put a little butter in a large frying pan/skillet set over medium heat. Allow the butter to melt and coat the base of the pan, then ladle a small amount of the rested batter into the pan and quickly spread it out very thinly. You can do this either by tilting the pan, or, for best results, use a crêpe swizzle stick. Cook until the top of the pancake is set then turn over carefully with a spatula and cook on the other side for a further 1–2 minutes until the crêpe is golden brown. Keep the crêpes warm while you cook the remaining batter in the same way.

To serve, set the pancakes in a small bowls or cups to form a basket shape. It is best to do this just after they are cooked and still warm. Fill with a generous amount of the cherry filling and a scoop of vanilla ice cream. Spoon the cream into the piping bag and pipe a swirl of cream on top. Sprinkle with the toasted almonds, transfer to a serving plate and serve immediately.

apple crêpes

My Great-Aunt Meg used to make us apple-filled pancakes whenever we went to visit her in Wales when we were children. They were so delicious that I still remember their taste today. Served with whipped cream, these are one of my favourite desserts.

140 g/1 cup plain/all-purpose flour, sifted

1 egg and 1 egg yolk

2 tablespoons melted butter, cooled, plus extra for frying

15 g/1 heaped tablespoon caster/granulated sugar

a pinch of salt

1 teaspoon ground cinnamon

300 ml/1¼ cups milk

250 ml/1 cup double/heavy cream, whipped to stiff peaks, to serve

icing sugar/confectioners' sugar, to dust

FOR THE APPLE COMPOTE
6 eating apples, peeled, cored and cut into small pieces

60 g/½ cup sultanas/golden raisins

1 teaspoon ground cinnamon, plus extra for dusting

100 g/½ cup caster/granulated sugar

125 ml/½ cup water

a large frying pan/skillet, griddle or crêpe pan/machine

a crêpe swizzle stick (optional)

Makes 10

Begin by preparing the apple compote. Put all of the ingredients in a saucepan or pot set over a medium heat and simmer for 15–20 minutes until the apple is soft. Set aside to cool.

To make the crêpe batter, put the flour, egg and egg yolk, melted butter, caster/granulated sugar, salt and cinnamon in a large mixing bowl. Whisking all the time, gradually add the milk until you have a smooth and runny batter. Cover and put the batter in the refrigerator to rest for 30 minutes.

When you are ready to serve, remove the batter from the refrigerator and stir gently. Put a little butter in a large frying pan/skillet set over medium heat. Allow the butter to melt and coat the base of the pan, then ladle a small amount of the rested batter into the pan and quickly spread it out very thinly. You can do this either by tilting the pan, or, for best results, use a crêpe swizzle stick. Cook until the top of the pancake is set then turn over carefully with a spatula and cook on the other side for a further 1–2 minutes until the crêpe is golden brown. Keep the crêpes warm while you cook the remaining batter.

Spoon the apple compote and a little whipped cream onto one half of each crêpe, then top with a handful of the reserved whole raspberries. Fold the crêpe in half and then half again.

Dust with ground cinnamon and icing/confectioners' sugar and serve.

tropical crêpes

When on beach holidays, there is nothing I like more than sipping an ice-cold piña colada — the inspiration for these crêpes with a warm pineapple and coconut sauce. You can add a little coconut rum to the sauce to be true to the cocktail, if you wish. You can replace the fresh pineapple with drained, tinned pineapple, although you can't beat the taste of the fresh fruit!

180 g/1½ cups plain/all-purpose flour, sifted

1 egg and 1 egg yolk

2 tablespoons melted butter, cooled, plus extra for frying

1 tablespoon caster/granulated sugar

a pinch of salt

250 ml/1 cup milk

160 ml/⅔ cup coconut milk

40 g/½ cup long shredded soft coconut/desiccated coconut, to serve

500 g/4 cups tropical fruits (mango, pomegranate, physalis in any combination of your choosing), to fill

FOR THE SAUCE

400 g/2⅔ cups peeled and sliced fresh pineapple

100 ml/⅓ cup water

250 ml/1 cup coconut milk

100 g/½ cup caster/granulated sugar

a large frying pan/skillet, griddle or crêpe pan/machine

a crêpe swizzle stick (optional)

Makes 10

To make the crêpe batter, put the flour, egg and egg yolk, melted butter, caster/granulated sugar and salt in a large mixing bowl. Whisking all the time, gradually add the milk and coconut milk until you have a smooth and runny batter. Cover and put the batter in the refrigerator to rest for 30 minutes.

While the batter is resting, make the sauce. Put 300 g/2 cups of the pineapple in a food processor with the water and pulse to a smooth pulp. Transfer the pineapple purée to a saucepan or pot and add the coconut milk and sugar. Simmer over a medium heat until the sugar has dissolved and the sauce is syrupy. Keep the pan on the heat but turn it down to low to keep the sauce warm until you are ready to serve.

For the coconut topping, toast the shredded coconut in a dry frying pan/skillet set over a high heat until it is lightly golden brown, watching it very carefully as it can burn easily. Set aside until you are ready to serve.

Remove the batter from the refrigerator and stir gently. Put a little butter in a large frying pan/skillet set over medium heat. Allow the butter to melt and coat the base of the pan, then ladle a small amount of the rested batter into the pan and quickly spread the batter out very thinly. You can do this either by tilting the pan, or, for best results, use a crêpe swizzle stick. Cook until the top of the pancake is set then turn over carefully with a spatula and cook on the other side for a further 1–2 minutes until the crêpe is golden brown. Keep the crêpes warm while you cook the remaining batter.

To serve the crêpes, put some of the reserved pineapple and tropical fruits in the centre of each crêpe and pour over the warm coconut sauce. Fold the edges of the crêpe into a fan shape, then sprinkle with the toasted coconut and serve immediately.

crêpes suzette

Crêpes Suzette are an extravagant, yet simple to prepare, dessert. I still remember the first time I ate them and being wowed by the waiter as he spectacularly flambéed them in front of us at the table. With a citrus sauce flavoured with liqueur (usually Grand Marnier) and ignited when served, these crêpes add an element of drama to any occasion.

140 g/1 cup plain/all-purpose flour, sifted

1 egg and 1 egg yolk

2 tablespoons melted butter, cooled, plus extra for frying

15 g/1 heaped tablespoon caster/granulated sugar

a pinch of salt

1 teaspoon vanilla extract/vanilla bean paste

300 ml/1¼ cups milk

FOR THE SAUCE

freshly squeezed juice of 3 large oranges, the grated zest of 1 orange

freshly squeezed juice of 2 lemons, the grated zest of 1 lemon

2 tablespoons caster/granulated sugar

2 tablespoons butter

3–4 tablespoons Grand Marnier or other orange liqueur

a sauce bottle fitted with a small, round nozzle/tip

a large frying pan/skillet, griddle or crêpe pan/machine

Makes 10

To make the crêpe batter, put the flour, egg and egg yolk, melted butter, caster/granulated sugar, salt and vanilla extract/vanilla bean paste in a large mixing bowl. Whisking all the time, gradually add the milk until you have a smooth and runny batter. Cover and put the batter in the refrigerator to rest for 30 minutes.

While the batter is resting, make the sauce. Put the grated orange and lemon zest and the juice from all the oranges and lemons into a large saucepan or pot set over a medium heat. Add the sugar, butter and 2 tablespoons of the Grand Marnier and simmer until the butter and sugar have dissolved.

When you are ready to serve, remove the batter from the refrigerator and stir gently. Transfer the batter to the sauce bottle. Put a little butter in a large frying pan/skillet set over medium heat. Allow the butter to melt and coat the base of the pan, then, using the sauce bottle, quickly drizzle connecting swirls of batter into the pan. Cook until the top of the crêpe is set then turn over very carefully with a spatula and cook on the other side for a further 1–2 minutes until the crêpe is golden brown. Keep the crêpes warm while you cook the remaining crêpes.

Put the remaining Grand Marnier in a separate frying pan/skillet set over a medium heat. Fold the crêpes in half and half again and place into the frying pan/skillet to coat them in the sauce. Once warm, carefully ignite the liqueur and add the orange sauce to flambé.

Serve immediately with the sauce poured over the top.

pumpkin chiffon crêpes

*My American friend, Marie Globus, makes the best pumpkin pie I know —
her pie is the inspiration for these crêpes, which are the perfect autumnal
dessert, with hints of cinnamon, ginger and vanilla.*

140 g/1 cup plain/all-purpose flour,
sifted

1 egg and 1 egg yolk

2 tablespoons melted butter, cooled,
plus extra for frying

15 g/1 heaped tablespoon
caster/granulated sugar

1 teaspoon vanilla extract/vanilla
bean paste

2 tablespoons pumpkin purée (such
as Libby's)

a pinch of salt

300 ml/1¼ cups milk

300 ml/1¼ cups double/heavy
cream, whipped to stiff peaks,
to serve

70 g/¾ cup pecans, finely chopped,
to serve

FOR THE FILLING

250 g/2¼ cups pumpkin purée

3 eggs, separated

170 g/¾ cup caster/granulated sugar

250 ml/1 cup milk

a pinch of salt or vanilla salt

1 teaspoon ground ginger

a pinch of nutmeg

2 teaspoons ground cinnamon

1 teaspoon vanilla extract/vanilla
bean paste

2 tablespoons melted butter

10 g/3 teaspoons powdered gelatine

60 ml/¾ cup warm water

*a large frying pan/skillet, griddle or
crêpe pan/machine*

a crêpe swizzle stick (optional)

Makes 10

Begin by preparing the pumpkin filling. Put the pumpkin purée in a large
mixing bowl set over a saucepan pot of boiling water and cook for 10
minutes to remove some of the liquid from the purée. While still over the
heat, whisk in the egg yolks, 90 g/½ cup of the caster/granulated sugar and
all of the milk until you have a smooth mixture. Cook for a further 5
minutes then add the salt, ginger, nutmeg, cinnamon, vanilla extract/vanilla
bean paste and melted butter. Cook until the mixture thickens and sticks
to the back of a wooden spoon. Remove the bowl from the heat and set
aside. In a separate bowl, whisk the gelatine into the warm water until it
dissolves and then stir it into the pumpkin mixture. Cover and chill in the
refrigerator until the mixture has set, ideally overnight.

Once the pumpkin mixture has set, in a mixing bowl, whisk the egg
whites to stiff peaks and then whisk in the remaining 80 g/½ cup of
caster/granulated sugar, a tablespoonful at a time, whisking all the time
to make a stiff meringue. Beat the pumpkin mixture a little to loosen
it then fold the meringue into the pumpkin mixture. Chill until you are
ready to serve.

To make the crêpe batter, put the flour, egg and egg yolk, melted butter,
caster/granulated sugar, vanilla extract/vanilla bean paste, pumpkin purée
and salt in a large mixing bowl. Whisking all the time, gradually add the
milk until you have a smooth and runny batter. Cover and put the batter
in the refrigerator to rest for 30 minutes.

When you are ready to serve, remove the batter from the refrigerator and
stir gently. Put a little butter in a large frying pan/skillet set over medium
heat. Allow the butter to melt and coat the base of the pan, then ladle a
small amount of the rested batter into the pan. Cook until the batter on top
of the crêpe is set then turn over very carefully with a spatula and cook on
the other side for a further 1–2 minutes until the crêpe is golden brown.
Keep the crêpes warm while you cook the remaining batter in the same way.

To serve, put the crêpes in a small bowls or cups to form a basket
shape. It is best to do this just after they are cooked and still warm. Fill
with a generous spoonful of the pumpkin mixture and some whipped
cream. Sprinkle with the chopped pecans, transfer to a serving plate and
serve immediately.

rhubarb and custard crêpes

Tangy, pink rhubarb and creamy custard perfectly complement each other. This combination makes a great pancake filling with lashings of homemade custard to pour over. You can make both the rhubarb and custard in advance and cook the pancakes just before serving.

140 g/1 cup plain/all-purpose flour, sifted

1 egg and 1 egg yolk

2 tablespoons melted butter, cooled, plus extra for frying

15 g/1 heaped tablespoon caster/granulated sugar

a pinch of salt

300 ml/1¼ cups milk

icing sugar/confectioners' sugar, to dust

FOR THE ROASTED RHUBARB

800 g/20 sticks pink rhubarb, ends trimmed

2 tablespoons caster/granulated sugar

120 ml/½ cup water

FOR THE CUSTARD

4 egg yolks

80 g/½ cup caster/granulated sugar

2 level tablespoons cornflour/corn starch, sifted

1 vanilla pod/bean, halved and seeds removed (see Note)

300 ml/1¼ cups double/heavy cream

250 ml/1 cup milk

an ovenproof dish, greased

a large frying pan/skillet, griddle or crêpe pan/machine

a crêpe swizzle stick (optional)

Makes 10

Begin by preparing the roasted rhubarb. Preheat the oven to 170°C (325°F) Gas 3. Put the rhubarb in the prepared ovenproof dish. Sprinkle with the sugar and pour over the water. Bake in the preheated oven for 30–40 minutes until the rhubarb is soft but still holds its shape.

To make the crêpe batter, put the flour, egg and egg yolk, melted butter, caster/granulated sugar and salt in a large mixing bowl. Whisking all the time, gradually add the milk until you have a smooth and runny batter. Cover and put the batter in the refrigerator to rest for 30 minutes.

While the batter is resting, make the custard. Place the egg yolks, sugar and cornflour/corn starch in a mixing bowl and whisk until very light and creamy. Set aside. Put the prepared vanilla pod and seeds (see method below) in a saucepan or pot with the cream and milk set over a high heat. Bring to the boil and then, whisking continuously, pour the hot milk over the egg mixture. Whisk well and then return to the pan. Stir over a gentle heat for a few minutes, until the custard starts to thicken. Remove the vanilla pod and leave to cool.

Remove the batter from the refrigerator and stir gently. Put a little butter in a large frying pan/skillet set over medium heat. Allow the butter to melt and coat the base of the pan, then ladle a small amount of the rested batter into the pan. Cook until the top of the crêpe is set then turn over very carefully with a spatula and cook on the other side for a further 1–2 minutes until the crêpe is golden brown. Keep the crêpes warm while you cook the remaining batter in the same way.

Fill each crêpe with a little custard and 2 sticks of roasted rhubarb, then roll up.

Dust with icing sugar and serve with the remaining custard on the side.

Note

To prepare vanilla pods/beans for use in cooking, simply cut in half and run the back of a knife along the pod halves to remove the seeds. The pod can be used alone, with the seeds or seeds only. Once used, the pod can be washed, dried and then stored in a sterilized jar filled with caster/granulated sugar to make vanilla sugar.

chocolate mint crêpes

After Eight mints make a rich and indulgent sauce for these crêpes. If you really love peppermint, then serve with mint choc chip ice cream, but I prefer good quality vanilla ice cream because it really enhances the flavour of the mint.

120 g/1 cup plain/all-purpose flour, sifted

30 g/3½ tablespoons cocoa powder

1 egg and 1 egg yolk

2 tablespoons melted butter, cooled, plus extra for frying

15 g/1 heaped tablespoon caster/granulated sugar

a pinch of salt

350 ml/1½ cups milk

10 scoops vanilla ice cream or mint choc-chip ice cream, to serve

20 After Eight chocolates or other fondant-filled mints, to serve

icing sugar/confectioners' sugar, to dust

FOR THE SAUCE

200 ml/¾ cup double/heavy cream

150 g/17 After Eight chocolates or other fondant-filled mints

a large frying pan/skillet, griddle or crêpe pan/machine

a crêpe swizzle stick (optional)

Makes 10

To make the crêpe batter, put the flour, cocoa powder, egg and egg yolk, melted butter, caster/granulated sugar and salt in a large mixing bowl. Whisking all the time, gradually add the milk until you have a smooth and runny batter. Cover and put the batter in the refrigerator to rest for 30 minutes.

While the batter is resting, make the chocolate mint sauce. Heat the cream and chocolate mints in a saucepan or pot set over a medium heat until the chocolate mints have melted. Keep the pan on the heat but turn it down to low to keep the sauce warm until you are ready to serve.

Remove the batter from the refrigerator and stir gently. Put a little butter in a large frying pan/skillet set over medium heat. Allow the butter to melt and coat the base of the pan, then ladle a small amount of the rested batter into the pan and quickly spread the batter out very thinly. You can do this either by tilting the pan, or, for best results, use a crêpe swizzle stick. Cook until the top of the pancake is set then turn over carefully with a spatula and cook on the other side for a further 1–2 minutes until the crêpe is crispy. Keep the crêpes warm while you cook the remaining batter.

Place a spoonful or two of the chocolate mint sauce onto each crêpe and top with a scoop of ice cream and a few chocolate mints then fold the crêpes in half. Dust with icing/confectioners' sugar and serve immediately.

soufflé crêpes

These crêpes make a most impressive dessert! You can vary the flavour of the soufflé easily, but this is my favourite recipe — with hints of vanilla and lemon served with mint-infused strawberries on the side. This is my idea of heaven!

140 g/1 cup plain/all-purpose flour, sifted

1 egg and 1 egg yolk

15 g/1 heaped tablespoon caster/granulated sugar

2 tablespoons melted butter, cooled, plus extra for frying

a pinch of salt

300 ml/1¼ cups milk

icing/confectioners' sugar, to dust

FOR THE STRAWBERRIES AND SYRUP

400 g/4 cups strawberries, hulled and halved

1 tablespoon finely chopped mint

1 tablespoon caster/granulated sugar

1 tablespoon lemon and mint cordial

FOR THE SOUFFLÉ

30 g/¼ cup plain/all-purpose flour, sifted

1 teaspoon finely grated lemon zest

250 ml/1 cup milk

90 g/½ cup caster/superfine sugar

½ teaspoon vanilla salt or ½ teaspoon sea salt plus 1 teaspoon vanilla extract/vanilla bean paste

4 eggs, separated plus 1 egg white (spare from the crêpe recipe above)

1 tablespoon butter

½ teaspoon cream of tartar

1 teaspoon vanilla sugar (see Note on page 57)

a large frying pan/skillet, griddle or crêpe pan/machine

a crêpe swizzle stick (optional)

a large baking sheet, lined with a silicon mat or baking parchment

Makes 6

Begin by preparing the strawberries and syrup. Put all of the ingredients in a mixing bowl. Stir well and leave to chill in the refrigerator for a few hours, stirring occasionally, until the sugar has dissolved.

Make the crêpe batter following the method on page 36.

For the soufflé, put the flour and lemon zest in a mixing bowl. Then put the milk, 40 g/¼ cup of the caster/granulated sugar and vanilla salt in a saucepan or pot set over a high heat and bring to the boil. Add a quarter of the heated milk to the flour and mix well until you have a smooth paste. Then gradually add the remainder of the milk. Whisk in the egg yolks and the butter to make a custard and set aside until cool.

Preheat the oven to 200°C (400°F) Gas 5.

Remove the batter from the refrigerator and stir gently. Put a little butter in a large frying pan/skillet set over medium heat. Allow the butter to melt and coat the base of the pan, then ladle a small amount of the rested batter into the pan and quickly spread the batter out very thinly. You can do this either by tilting the pan, or, for best results, use a crêpe swizzle stick. The crêpes need to be about 25 cm/10 inch in diameter otherwise they will not be large enough to fold up the soufflé. Cook until the top of the pancake is set then turn over carefully with a spatula and cook on the other side for a further 1–2 minutes until the crêpe is golden brown. The crêpes do not need to be kept warm while you cook the remaining batter.

In a clean, dry bowl whisk the 5 egg whites to stiff peaks. Add the remaining 50 g/¼ cup of caster/granulated sugar gradually, whisking all the time. Add the cream of tartar and vanilla sugar and whisk in.

Fold a quarter of the meringue mixture into the cooled custard. Then gently fold in the remaining meringue. Lay one of the crêpes on a large plate and spread a sixth of the soufflé mixture over half of the crêpe. Fold the other half of the crêpe over the soufflé mixture and then fold in half again. Place the souffle-filled crêpe on the prepared baking sheet. Repeat with the remaining crêpes, bake in the preheated oven for 10–15 minutes until the soufflés have risen and are lightly golden brown.

Dust with icing/confectioners' sugar and serve immediately with the strawberries and their syrup.

waffles

vanilla waffles with vanilla syrup

It is really worth using vanilla pods for their flavour in this recipe. Their tiny black seeds float delicately in the vanilla syrup and make a perfect topping for these waffles.

260 g/2 cups self-raising/rising flour, sifted

1 teaspoon vanilla extract/vanilla bean paste

60 g/scant ⅓ cup caster/granulated sugar

a pinch of salt

3 eggs, separated

375 ml/1½ cups milk

60 g/4 tablespoons butter, melted

clotted cream, to serve

FOR THE SYRUP

1 vanilla pod/bean, halved and seeds removed (see Note)

250 ml/1 cup water

150 g/¾ cup caster/granulated sugar

an electric or stove-top waffle iron

Makes 8

Begin by making the syrup. Put the vanilla pod/bean and seeds, the water and the caster/granulated sugar in a saucepan or pot set over a medium heat. Simmer until you have a thin syrup then remove from the heat and set aside to cool.

To make the waffle batter, put the flour, vanilla extract/vanilla bean paste, caster/granulated sugar, salt, egg yolks, milk and melted butter in a large mixing bowl. Whisk until you have a smooth batter. In a separate mixing bowl, whisk the egg whites to stiff peaks and then gently fold into the batter a third at a time.

Preheat the waffle iron and grease with a little butter.

Ladle a small amount of the batter into the preheated waffle iron and cook the waffles for 3–5 minutes until golden brown. Keep the waffles warm while you cook the remaining batter in the same way.

Serve the waffles with the vanilla syrup and a spoonful of clotted cream.

Note

To prepare vanilla pods/beans for use in cooking, simply cut in half and run the back of a knife along the pod halves to remove the seeds. The pod can be used alone, with the seeds or seeds only. Once used, the pod can be washed, dried and then stored in a sterilized jar filled with caster/granulated sugar to make vanilla sugar.

apricot and white chocolate waffles

Apricot and white chocolate go perfectly together. These waffles are bursting with apricot pieces and white chocolate chips, and are served with roasted apricots and an apricot butter. A complete apricot overload!

260 g/2 cups self-raising/rising flour, sifted

60 g/scant ⅓ cup caster/granulated sugar

a pinch of salt

3 eggs, separated

375 ml/1½ cups milk

1 tablespoon apricot jam/jelly

60 g/4 tablespoons butter, melted

100 g/⅔ cup white chocolate chips

80 g/½ cup dried apricots, finely chopped

icing/confectioners' sugar, to dust

FOR THE ROASTED APRICOTS AND APRICOT BUTTER

600 g/4 cups fresh apricots, halved and stones/pits removed

50 g/¼ cup caster/granulated sugar

50 g/3½ tablespoons butter

an electric or stove-top waffle iron

an ovenproof roasting dish, greased

Makes 8

Begin by preparing the apricots. Preheat the oven to 180ºC (350ºF) Gas 4. Cut the apricots in half and remove the stones/pits. Place the apricot halves, cut side down, in the prepared roasting dish and sprinkle over the sugar. Cut the butter into small pieces and dot over the apricots. Bake in the preheated oven for about 25–30 minutes until the fruit is soft but still holds its shape. Remove from the oven then purée half of the apricots and the juices from the dish in a food processor until smooth to form the apricot butter. Set aside together with remaining halved apricots until you are ready to serve.

To make the waffle batter, put the flour, caster/granulated sugar, salt, egg yolks, milk, apricot jam/jelly and melted butter in a large mixing bowl. Whisk until you have a smooth batter. In a separate mixing bowl, whisk the egg whites to stiff peaks and then gently fold into the batter a third at a time. Fold in the white chocolate chips and dried apricot pieces.

Preheat the waffle iron and grease with a little butter.

Ladle a small amount of the batter into the preheated waffle iron and cook the waffles for 3–5 minutes until golden brown. Keep the waffles warm while you cook the remaining batter in the same way, stirring the batter each time to mix in the apricot pieces and chocolate chips.

Serve the waffles immediately, dusted with icing/confectioners' sugar, with the roasted apricots and apricot butter.

salted caramel waffles

Salted caramel gives these waffles a modern twist. I could eat the sauce on its own but it is delicious with caramel waffles and chocolate curls. The recipe calls for vanilla salt which is available from good delicatessens or online but if you want you can make your own at home following the method here.

260 g/2 cups self-raising/rising flour, sifted

1 teaspoon baking powder

3 eggs, separated

375 ml/1½ cups milk

75 g/5 tablespoons butter, melted, plus extra for greasing

50 g/½ cup plain/bittersweet chocolate curls, to serve

FOR THE SALTED CARAMEL SAUCE

150 g/¾ cup caster/granulated sugar

100 g/7 tablespoons butter

1 teaspoon vanilla salt (see Note) or sea salt plus 1 teaspoon vanilla extract/vanilla bean paste

250 ml/1 cup double/heavy cream

an electric or stove-top waffle iron

Makes 8

Begin by making the salted caramel sauce. Put the sugar and butter in a saucepan or pot set over a medium heat and simmer until both have melted and the resulting caramel starts to turn a deep golden brown colour. Add the salt and cream and whisk over the heat until the sauce is smooth and glossy. If any lumps of sugar have formed in your sauce, strain through a fine mesh sieve/strainer over a mixing bowl. Set aside to cool.

To make the waffle batter, put the flour, baking powder, egg yolks, milk and melted butter in a large mixing bowl. Whisk until you have a smooth batter. Add 80 ml/scant ⅓ cup of the caramel sauce and whisk again. In a separate mixing bowl, whisk the egg whites to stiff peaks and then gently fold into the batter a third at a time.

Preheat the waffle iron and grease with a little butter.

Ladle a small amount of the batter into the preheated waffle iron and cook the waffles for 3–5 minutes until golden brown. Keep the waffles warm while you cook the remaining batter in the same way.

Serve the waffles immediately with the caramel sauce on the side, topped with chocolate curls.

Note

To make vanilla salt, split 2 vanilla pods/vanilla beans and remove the seeds. Cut the pods in half. Stir the vanilla seeds into several large spoonfuls of sea salt flakes. Place the salt, seeds and vanilla pods/vanilla beans in a sterilized airtight jar and set aside for 2 weeks. Discard the vanilla pods/vanilla beans before using.

pistachio waffles

I made these waffles one sunny, summer's afternoon with three lovely children; Hector, Rosie and Felix. Hector was a very good sous-chef and perfectly folded in the egg whites. The results were delicious! Pistachio ice cream has a delicate, perfumed flavour and is a great accompaniment to the nutty waffles. If you are short of time you can use store-bought pistachio or vanilla ice cream instead.

100 g/¾ cup pistachios, plus a handful finely chopped, to garnish

240 g/scant 2 cups self-raising/rising flour, sifted

60 g/scant ⅓ cup caster/granulated sugar

a pinch of salt

3 eggs, separated

375 ml/1½ cups milk

60 g/4 tablespoons butter, melted

FOR THE ICE CREAM

100 g/¾ cup pistachios

400 ml/1⅔ cup double/heavy cream

200 ml/¾ cup milk

5 egg yolks

100 g/½ cup caster/granulated sugar

FOR THE SAUCE

200 g/1⅓ cup white chocolate

250 ml/1 cup double/heavy cream

an electric or stove-top waffle iron

an ice cream machine (optional, see Note on page 74)

Makes 8

Begin by preparing the ice cream. Put the pistachios in a food processor and pulse to a fine crumb. Transfer the finely ground pistachios to a saucepan or pot set over a high heat with the double/heavy cream and milk. Bring the mixture to the boil, then remove from the heat and leave to infuse for 30 minutes. In a mixing bowl, whisk together the egg yolks and caster/granulated sugar until very thick and pale yellow in colour. Return the pistachio milk to the heat and bring to the boil again. Pour the boiling pistachio milk over the eggs in a thin stream, whisking all the time. Return the mixture to the pan and cook for a few minutes longer until it begins to thicken. Leave to cool completely. Then churn in an ice cream machine following the instructions on page 74 or the manufacturer's instructions. Transfer to a freezer-proof container and store in the freezer until you are ready to serve.

For the sauce, put the white chocolate and double/heavy cream in a saucepan or pot set over a medium heat and simmer until the chocolate has melted, stirring all the time. Keep the pan on the heat but turn it down to low to keep the sauce warm until you are ready to serve.

To make the waffle batter, put the pistachios in a food processor and pulse to a fine crumb. Place the pistachios in a large mixing bowl with the flour, sugar, salt, egg yolks, milk and melted butter. Whisk until you have a smooth batter. In a separate mixing bowl, whisk the egg whites to stiff peaks and then gently fold into the batter a third at a time.

Preheat the waffle iron and grease with a little butter.

Ladle a small amount of the batter into the preheated waffle iron and cook the waffles for 2–3 minutes until golden brown. Keep the waffles warm while you cook the remaining batter in the same way.

Serve the waffles drizzled with the white chocolate sauce, topped with generous scoops of ice cream and decorated with the chopped pistachios.

s'mores waffles

Traditional s'mores use digestives biscuits/graham crackers to sandwich toasted marshmallows and chocolate together — a campsite classic! My waffle version is rich, indulgent and utterly delicious. They are definitely big enough to share — I have never known anyone to manage a whole one on their own!

260 g/2 cups self-raising/rising flour, sifted

20 g/2½ tablespoons cocoa powder, sifted

60 g/scant ⅓ cup caster/granulated sugar

a pinch of salt

3 eggs, separated

375 ml/1½ cups milk

60 g/4 tablespoons butter, melted

about 40 large marshmallows

200 g/1⅓ cup plain/bittersweet chocolate, cut into chunks, plus extra, melted, to serve

an electric or stove-top waffle iron
a chef's blow torch

Makes 4

To make the waffle batter, put the flour, cocoa powder, caster/granulated sugar, salt, egg yolks, milk and melted butter in a large mixing bowl. Whisk until you have a smooth batter. In a separate mixing bowl, whisk the egg whites to stiff peaks and then gently fold into the batter a third at a time.

Preheat the waffle iron and grease with a little butter.

Ladle a small amount of the batter into the preheated waffle iron and cook for 2–3 minutes until crisp. Cook a second waffle in the same way.

Meanwhile cut 10 marshmallows in half and place them on top of the cooked waffle. Using the blow torch, toast the tops of the marshmallows until they are golden brown and soft. If you do not have a chef's blow torch you can toast the marshmallows under a grill. Place a quarter of the chocolate chunks on top of the toasted marshmallows, then place a second hot waffle on top and serve immediately. You need the heat of the second waffle to melt the chocolate so you need to make and serve these as you go along. Repeat with the remaining ingredients until all the batter is used up.

Serve with extra melted chocolate drizzled over.

peanut waffles with snickers ice cream

For peanut lovers, these waffles are a super treat. Bursting with peanut flavour and served with peanut butter and chocolate ice cream and Snickers sauce, they are certainly not for the faint-hearted or calorie conscious! Adding honey to the sauce takes away some of the sweetness.

225 g/1¾ cups self-raising/rising flour, sifted

1 teaspoon baking powder

2 tablespoon caster/granulated sugar

3 eggs, separated

400 ml/1⅔ cups milk

2 tablespoons smooth peanut butter

100 g/7 tablespoons butter, melted

FOR THE ICE CREAM

400 ml/1⅔ cups double/heavy cream

200 ml/¾ cups milk

5 egg yolks

100 g/½ cup caster/granulated sugar

2 tablespoons peanut butter (crunchy or smooth)

FOR THE SAUCE

400 ml/1⅔ cups double/heavy cream

6 Snickers bars or other nut, caramel and nougat chocolate bar, chopped

2 teaspoons clear honey

an electric or stove-top waffle iron

an ice cream machine (optional, see Note)

Makes 8

Begin by preparing the sauce. Place the cream, Snickers bars and honey in a saucepan or pot set over a medium heat and simmer until the Snickers bars have melted and the sauce is glossy. Set aside to cool.

For the ice cream, put the double/heavy cream and milk in a saucepan or pot set over a high heat and bring to the boil. In a mixing bowl, whisk together the egg yolks and caster/granulated sugar until very thick and pale yellow in colour. Pour the hot milk over the eggs in a thin stream, whisking all the time. Add the peanut butter and whisk again. Return the mixture to the pan and cook for a few minutes longer, until it begins to thicken. Leave to cool completely. Then churn in an ice cream machine following the manufacturer's instructions. Once the ice cream is almost frozen, but still soft enough to stir, stir through about a third of the chocolate peanut sauce so that it is rippled through the ice cream. Transfer to a freezer-proof container and store in the freezer until you are ready to serve.

To make the waffle batter, put the flour, baking powder, caster/granulated sugar, salt, egg yolks, milk, peanut butter and melted butter in a large mixing bowl. Whisk until you have a smooth batter. In a separate mixing bowl, whisk the egg whites to stiff peaks and then gently fold into the batter a third at a time.

Preheat the waffle iron and grease with a little butter.

Ladle a small amount of the batter into the preheated waffle iron and cook the waffles for 2–3 minutes until golden brown. Keep the waffles warm while you cook the remaining batter in the same way.

Serve the waffles immediately with the ice cream and remaining sauce.

Note

If you do not have an ice cream machine, place the mixture in a freezer-proof container in the freezer and whisk every 20 minutes or so until frozen to break up the ice crystals. The ice cream can be stored for up to 3 months in the freezer.

orange waffles with roasted plums

Roasted plums made by my lovely Grandma was something I often ate for dessert when I was young. Such a simple dessert, but deliciously tangy, they are served here with orange and vanilla waffles and lashings of clotted cream.

260 g/2 cups self-raising/rising flour, sifted

1 teaspoon orange zest

3 eggs, separated

375 ml/1½ cups milk

1 teaspoon vanilla extract/vanilla bean paste

2 tablespoons caster/granulated sugar

a pinch of salt

60 g/4 tablespoons butter, melted

clotted cream, to serve

icing/confectioners' sugar, to dust

FOR THE ROASTED PLUMS

8 plums, halved and stones/pits removed

75 g/⅓ cup caster/granulated sugar

2 tablespoons water

freshly squeezed juice of 2 oranges

an ovenproof dish, greased

an electric or stove-top waffle iron

Makes 8

Begin by preparing the plums. Preheat the oven to 180°C (350°F) Gas 4. Put the plum halves, cut side down, in the prepared roasting dish and sprinkle over 25 g/2 tablespoons sugar, the water and the orange juice. Bake in the preheated oven for 20 minutes until the fruit is soft but still holds its shape. Remove the plums from the dish and pour the cooking liquid into a saucepan or pot set over a medium heat. Simmer with 50 g/¼ cup of the caster/granulated sugar and 60 ml/¼ cup more water until you have a thin syrup. Set aside together with removed halved plums until you are ready to serve.

To make the waffle batter, put the flour, orange zest, egg yolks, milk, vanilla extract/vanilla bean paste, caster/granulated sugar, salt and melted butter into a large mixing bowl. Whisk until you have a smooth batter. In a separate mixing bowl, whisk the egg whites to stiff peaks and then gently fold into the batter a third at a time. Fold in the white chocolate chips and dried apricots.

Preheat the waffle iron and grease with a little butter.

Ladle a small amount of the batter into the preheated waffle iron and cook the waffles for 2–3 minutes until golden brown. Keep the waffles warm while you cook the remaining batter in the same way.

Dust the waffles with icing/confectioners' sugar and serve immediately with the roasted plums, plum syrup and clotted cream.

lemon waffles

These lemony waffles are topped with homemade lemon curd. I often make a double quantity of lemon curd so that I have extra in the fridge for an emergency citrus fix!

260 g/2 cups self-raising/rising flour, sifted

1 teaspoon baking powder

60 g/scant ⅓ cup caster/granulated sugar

a pinch of salt

3 eggs, separated

375 ml/1½ cups milk

75 g/5 tablespoons butter, melted

crème fraîche, to serve

icing/confectioners' sugar, for dusting

FOR THE LEMON CURD

freshly squeezed juice and grated zest of 2 unwaxed lemons, the zest of 1 lemon reserved for the waffle batter

freshly squeezed juice and grated zest of 1 unwaxed lime

60 g/4 tablespoons butter

120 g/heaped ½ cup caster/granulated sugar

2 eggs

an electric or stove-top waffle iron

Makes 8

Begin by making the lemon curd. Put the zest of 1 lemon in a heatproof bowl set over a saucepan or pot of simmering water. Add the lemon and lime juice, the butter and caster/granulated sugar. Simmer until the butter has melted and the sugar has dissolved and remove from the heat. In a separate mixing bowl, beat the eggs and stir 1 tablespoon at a time into the lemon butter mixture, whisking after each addition. Return the mixture to the heat and stir for a further 10–15 minutes until the curd is thick. Set aside to cool until you are ready to serve, then store in a sterilized jar in the refrigerator for up to 1 month.

To make the waffle batter, put the flour, reserved lemon zest, baking powder, caster/granulated sugar, salt, egg yolks, milk and melted butter in a large mixing bowl. Whisk until you have a smooth batter. In a separate mixing bowl, whisk the egg whites to stiff peaks and then gently fold into the batter a third at a time.

Preheat the waffle iron and grease with a little butter.

Ladle a small amount of the batter into the preheated waffle iron and cook the waffles for 2–3 minutes until golden brown. Keep the waffles warm while you cook the remaining batter in the same way.

Serve the waffles immediately with the lemon curd and a dollop of crème fraîche. Dust with icing/confectioners' sugar and enjoy!

pecan praline waffles

Making praline is not difficult and the results are so delicious. Caramelizing sugar takes a little patience but once melted the golden caramel mixes beautifully with the pecans to give a nutty crunch. It's great whipped into cream or for sprinkling over these waffles.

240 g/scant 2 cups self-raising/
rising flour, sifted

60 g/scant ⅓ cup caster/granulated
sugar

a pinch of salt

3 eggs, separated

375 ml/1½ cups milk

100 g/½ cup pecans, finely chopped

60 g/4 tablespoons butter, melted

250 ml/2 cups double/heavy cream,
to serve

maple syrup, to serve

FOR THE PRALINE

100 g/½ cup pecan nuts

100 g/½ cup caster/granulated
sugar

an electric or stove-top waffle iron

*a baking sheet lined with baking
parchment and greased, or a
silicon mat*

Makes 8

Begin by making the praline. Heat the sugar in a dry saucepan or pot set over a medium heat until it melts and turns golden brown. Do not stir the sugar but swirl it from time to time to prevent it from burning. Scatter the pecans onto the prepared baking sheet then pour the sugar caramel over the nuts and leave to set. Once cool, transfer the praline sheet to a food processor and pulse to a fine crumb. Store in an airtight container until you are ready to serve. The praline is best made on the day you are using it as it can become sticky when exposed to the air.

To make the waffle batter, put the flour, caster/granulated sugar, salt, egg yolks, milk, chopped pecans and melted butter in a large mixing bowl. Whisk until you have a smooth batter. In a separate mixing bowl, whisk the egg whites to stiff peaks and then gently fold into the batter a third at a time.

Preheat the waffle iron and grease with a little butter.

Ladle a small amount of the batter into the preheated waffle iron and cook the waffles for 2–3 minutes until golden brown. Keep the waffles warm while you cook the remaining batter in the same way.

Put the cream in a bowl with half of the praline and whisk to stiff peaks.

Serve the waffles with a spoonful of praline cream, drizzled with maple syrup and sprinkled with the remaining pecan praline.

cinnamon waffles with cinnamon cream sauce

Cinnamon is a wonderfully versatile spice. Deliciously warming and rich it transforms the flavour of these waffles in an instant. Served with a buttery cinnamon sauce and cinnamon ice cream, they make great after dinner waffles.

260 g/2 cups self-raising/rising flour, sifted

1 teaspoon ground cinnamon

1 teaspoon baking powder

60 g/scant ⅓ cup caster/granulated sugar

a pinch of salt

3 eggs, separated

375 ml/1½ cups milk

75 g/5 tablespoons butter, melted

cinnamon or vanilla ice cream, to serve

FOR THE SAUCE

60 g/4 tablespoons butter

100 g/½ cup caster/granulated sugar

2 teaspoons ground cinnamon

250 ml/2 cups double/heavy cream

an electric or stove-top waffle iron

Makes 8

Begin by making the sauce. Melt the butter and sugar in a saucepan or pot set over a medium heat, then add the cinnamon. Simmer until the sauce thickens and becomes syrupy then remove from the heat and cool for a few minutes. Whisk in the cream, then return the pan to the heat and cook for a few minutes longer, whisking all the time. Keep the pan on the heat but turn it down to low to keep the sauce warm until you are ready to serve.

To make the waffle batter, put the flour, cinnamon, baking powder, caster/granulated sugar, salt, egg yolks, milk and melted butter into a large mixing bowl. Whisk until you have a smooth batter. In a separate mixing bowl, whisk the egg whites to stiff peaks and then gently fold into the batter a third at a time.

Preheat the waffle iron and grease with a little butter.

Ladle a small amount of the batter into the preheated waffle iron and cook the waffles for 2–3 minutes until golden brown. Keep the waffles warm while you cook the remaining batter in the same way.

Serve the waffles immediately with scoops of ice cream and the hot cinnamon cream sauce poured over.

pear and ginger waffles

The piquant ginger spice runs throughout this recipe in its many forms — ground, stem, ginger syrup and ginger wine. If you love ginger, as I do, then this is the recipe for you. Although the poached pears are delicious, if you are short of time you can substitute sliced, fresh pears instead.

260 g/2 cups self-raising/rising flour, sifted

1 teaspoon ground ginger

60 g/scant ⅓ cup caster/granulated sugar

a pinch of salt

3 eggs, separated

375 ml/1½ cups milk

2 tablespoons ginger syrup

60 g/4 tablespoons butter, melted

icing/confectioners' sugar, to dust

ginger or maple syrup, to drizzle

FOR THE POACHED PEARS

4 ripe pears, peeled and cored, stalk intact

3 balls stem ginger preserved in syrup

80 ml/6 tablespoons ginger wine

2 tablespoons caster/granulated sugar

FOR THE CREAM

2 balls stem ginger, finely chopped, plus 1 tablespoon of the preserving ginger syrup

300 ml/1¼ cups double/heavy cream

an electric or stove-top waffle iron

Makes 8

Begin by preparing the pears. Put the pears in a saucepan or pot with the stem ginger, ginger wine and sugar and then add water to the pan until the pears are covered. Set over a medium heat and simmer for 20–30 minutes until the pears are soft. Drain the pears, discarding the liquid, and set aside to cool. Once cool, cut each pear in half, cutting through the stalk so that each pear half still has part of the stalk at the top. Thinly slice the pear but don't cut all the way through. This will mean that you can fan the pear out on top of the waffles. Set aside until you are ready to serve.

For the ginger cream, put the ginger syrup and cream in a mixing bowl and whip to soft peaks. Fold the ginger pieces into the mixture and store in the refrigerator until you are ready to serve.

To make the waffle batter, put the flour, ginger, caster/granulated sugar, salt, egg yolks, milk, ginger syrup and melted butter in a large mixing bowl. Whisk until you have a smooth batter. In a separate mixing bowl, whisk the egg whites to stiff peaks and then gently fold into the batter a third at a time.

Preheat the waffle iron and grease with a little butter.

Ladle a small amount of the batter into the preheated waffle iron and cook the waffles for 2–3 minutes until golden brown. Keep the waffles warm while you cook the remaining batter in the same way.

Serve the waffles immediately with a spoonful of the ginger cream and 1 poached pear half. Dust with icing/confectioners' sugar and drizzle with a little ginger syrup.

baileys waffles

Creamy, indulgent waffles with a hint of alcohol, these are perfect to make after a long, hard day when you need a treat to relax with. I love the simplicity of the creamy, boozy sauce, finished with a little clotted cream.

260 g/2 cups self-raising/rising flour, sifted

60 g/scant ⅓ cup caster/granulated sugar

80 ml/scant ⅓ cup Baileys or other cream liqueur

a pinch of salt

3 eggs, separated

300 ml/1¼ cups milk

60 g/4 tablespoons butter, melted

clotted cream, to serve

FOR THE SAUCE

100 ml/7 tablespoons Baileys or other cream liqueur

200 ml/¾ cup double/heavy cream

50 g/3½ tablespoons butter

a pinch of salt

50 g/¼ cup caster/granulated sugar

an electric or stove-top waffle iron

Makes 8

Begin by preparing the sauce. Put all of the ingredients in a saucepan or pot set over a medium heat and simmer until the sugar and butter melt and the sauce begins to thicken. Keep the pan on the heat but turn it down to low to keep the sauce warm until you are ready to serve.

To make the waffle batter, put the flour, caster/granulated sugar, Baileys, salt, egg yolks, milk and melted butter in a large mixing bowl. Whisk until you have a smooth batter. In a separate mixing bowl, whisk the egg whites to stiff peaks and then gently fold into the batter a third at a time.

Preheat the waffle iron and grease with a little butter.

Ladle a small amount of the batter into the preheated waffle iron and cook the waffles for 3–5 minutes until golden brown. Keep the waffles warm while you cook the remaining batter in the same way.

Serve the waffles with the warm Baileys sauce and a teaspoon of clotted cream per portion.

french toast

pain perdu with summer berries

One of my favourite tasks when I took part in Masterchef, was when we had to make breakfast for 10 people. Another contestant, Steven Wallis, and I chose to make this dish and it was a great success. Pain Perdu, 'lost bread', or more commonly known as 'egg bread', is so easy to make, and served with fresh berries and a summer berry sauce it is a very elegant breakfast.

2 eggs
60 ml/¼ cup double/heavy cream
1 tablespoon caster/granulated sugar
1–2 tablespoons butter, for frying
6 slices brioche or white bread

FOR THE SAUCE
200 g/2 cups strawberries
150 g/1 cup raspberries
150 ml/⅔ cup water
60 g/⅓ cup caster/granulated sugar

TO SERVE
150 g/1 cup raspberries, to serve
200 g/2 cups strawberries, to serve
crème fraîche, to serve
icing/confectioners' sugar, for dusting

a large frying pan/skillet or griddle
9-cm/3½-in circular cookie cutter

Serves 6

Begin by making the sauce. Put the strawberries and raspberries in a saucepan or pot with the water and sugar set over a medium heat. Simmer for 5 minutes until the fruit is very soft. Pass through a sieve/strainer over a bowl to remove the seeds and discard them. Set aside to cool.

For the pain perdu, whisk together the eggs, cream and sugar in a mixing bowl, transfer to a shallow dish and set aside. Melt the butter in a large frying pan/skillet set over a medium heat until the butter begins to foam. Use the cutter to cut out circles from the brioche. Soak each circle in the egg mixture on one side for a few seconds, then turn over and soak the other side. The bread should be fully coated in egg, but not too soggy – it is best to soak one slice at a time. Put each circle straight into the pan before soaking the next slice.

Cook for 2–3 minutes on each side until the brioche is golden brown. Keep the cooked brioche warm while you cook the remaining slices in the same way, adding a little butter to the pan each time, if required.

Serve the toasts warm, drizzled with the berry sauce, a few fresh berries and a generous spoonful of crème fraîche. Dust with icing/confectioners' sugar and enjoy!

cinnamon french toast

Cinnamon is my favourite spice. I love it in coffees, crumbles, cakes and cookies. It is used in abundance in this recipe as the bread is sandwiched together with a sweet cinnamon butter and the egg batter also contains ground cinnamon. These French toasts make a great, indulgent breakfast and can be served with fresh berries or stewed apple if you wish.

8 slices white bread, crusts removed

4 eggs

60 ml/¼ cup milk

2 teaspoons ground cinnamon

1 tablespoon caster/granulated sugar

1–2 tablespoons butter, for frying

sugar nibs/pearl sugar or caster/granulated sugar, for sprinkling

icing/confectioners' sugar, to dust

FOR THE FILLING

100 g/7 tablespoons butter, softened

1 teaspoon vanilla sugar (see Note on page 65)

50 g/¼ cup caster/granulated sugar

2 teaspoon ground cinnamon

a large frying pan/skillet or griddle

Serves 4

For the filling, mix together the butter, vanilla sugar, caster/granulated sugar and cinnamon to a smooth paste using a spoon or a fork.

Spread a thick layer of filling over 4 of the slices of bread and place a second slice of bread on top of each to sandwich the butter in the middle. Press the sandwiches down so that the filling will not leak.

For the French toast, whisk together the eggs, milk, cinnamon and sugar in a mixing bowl, transfer to a shallow dish and set aside. Melt the butter in a large frying pan/skillet set over a medium heat until the butter begins to foam. Soak each sandwich in the egg mixture on one side for a few seconds, then turn over and soak the other side. The bread should be fully coated in egg, but not too soggy – it is best to soak one sandwich at a time.

Put each sandwich straight into the frying pan/skillet with the melted butter set over a medium heat before soaking the next sandwich. Sprinkle the tops of the sandwiches with a little pearl sugar and cook for 2–3 minutes. Once the sandwiches are golden brown underneath, turn over and cook for a few minutes longer. The pearl sugar will caramelise and create a lightly crusty topping. Keep the cooked toast warm while you cook the remaining slices in the same way, adding a little butter to the pan each time, if required.

Serve immediately, sliced and dusted with icing/confectioners' sugar.

gingerbread french toast with lemon curd ice cream

Although traditionally made with bread or brioche, you can also make French toast with slices of cake. Served warm with lemon curd ice cream, this recipe makes an unusual after dinner dessert.

2 eggs

60 ml/¼ cup double/heavy cream

1 tablespoon caster/granulated sugar

1–2 tablespoons butter, for frying

8 slices of ginger cake (such as Jamaica Ginger cake)

icing/confectioners' sugar, to dust

FOR THE ICE CREAM

450 ml/1½ cup double/heavy cream

180 ml/¾ cup milk

5 egg yolks

90 g/scant ½ cup caster/granulated sugar

3 tablespoons lemon curd (see recipe on page 78)

an ice cream machine (optional, see Note on page 74)

a large frying pan/skillet or griddle

Serves 4

Begin by making the ice cream. Put the double/heavy cream and milk in a saucepan or pot set over a high heat and bring to the boil. In a mixing bowl, whisk together the egg yolks and caster/granulated sugar until very thick and pale yellow in colour. Pour the hot milk over the eggs in a thin stream, whisking all the time. Return the mixture to the pan and cook for a few minutes longer, until the custard begins to thicken. Leave to cool completely, then churn in an ice cream machine following the instructions on page 74 or the manufacturer's instructions. Once the ice cream is almost frozen, but still soft enough to stir, stir through the lemon curd so that it is rippled through the ice cream. Transfer to a freezer-proof container and store in the freezer until you are ready to serve.

For the gingerbread French toast, whisk together the eggs, cream and caster/granulated sugar in a mixing bowl, transfer to a shallow dish and set aside. Melt the butter in a large frying pan/skillet set over a medium heat until the butter begins to foam. Soak each slice of ginger cake in the egg mixture on one side for a few seconds, then turn over and soak the other side. The cake should be fully coated in egg, but not too soggy – it is best to soak one slice at a time. Put each slice straight into the pan before soaking the next slice.

Cook for 2–3 minutes on each side until the brioche is golden brown. Keep the cooked toast warm while you cook the remaining slices in the same way, adding a little butter to the pan each time, if required.

Serve the cake toasts warm with a scoop of ice cream, dusted with icing/confectioners' sugar.

strawberry and vanilla stuffed french toast

Light and delicate toasts, filled with ripe strawberries and mascarpone cheese and served with strawberry sauce, are one of the nicest things to make with a glut of ripe berries in the summer. You can use strawberries or raspberries (or both!) in this recipe.

4 thick slices of brioche or white bread

2 eggs

80 ml/scant ⅓ cup double/heavy cream

1 tablespoon caster/granulated sugar

1–2 tablespoons butter, for frying

icing/confectioners' sugar, to dust

FOR THE FILLING AND SAUCE

the seeds of ½ vanilla pod/vanilla bean (see Note on page 57)

125 g/scant 1 cup mascarpone cheese

225 g/scant 2 cups ripe strawberries

80 ml/scant ⅓ cup water

50 g/¼ cup caster/granulated sugar

a large frying pan/skillet or griddle

Serves 4

Begin by preparing the filling. Stir the vanilla seeds into the mascarpone cheese in a mixing bowl. Cut 5 strawberries into very small pieces and mix into the cheese.

For the sauce, place the remaining strawberries in a saucepan or pot with the water and sugar set over a medium heat. Simmer until the fruit is soft, then set aside to cool.

Using a sharp knife, cut a pocket in the top of each brioche slice to create a large cavity. Take care not to cut all the way through as it is this cavity which will hold your filling. Spoon a quarter of the mascarpone filling into each slice and press the opening down to close the pocket.

Whisk together the eggs, cream and caster/granulated sugar in a mixing bowl, transfer to a shallow dish and set aside. Melt the butter in a large frying pan/skillet set over a medium heat until the butter begins to foam. Soak each filled slice in the egg mixture on one side for a few seconds, then turn over and soak the other side. The slices should be fully coated in egg, but not too soggy – it is best to soak one slice at a time. Put each slice straight into the pan before soaking the next slice.

Cook for 2–3 minutes on each side until the brioche is golden brown. Keep the cooked toast warm while you cook the remaining slices in the same way, adding a little butter to the pan each time, if required.

Cut in half, dust with icing/confectioners' sugar and serve with the strawberries and their sauce.

pear and chocolate french toast

Poached pears are easy to prepare and often served as a classic dessert, Belle Hélène, with chocolate sauce and ice cream. That delicious dessert is the inspiration for these naughty, but very yummy, French toasts — bursting with soft pear and gooey chocolate which melts as the toasts are cooked.

4 large thick slices of crusty white bread

4 eggs

120 ml/½ cup double/heavy cream

2 tablespoons caster/granulated sugar, plus extra for sprinkling

1–2 tablespoons butter, for frying

icing/confectioners' sugar, for dusting (optional)

crème fraîche or vanilla ice cream, to serve

FOR THE FILLING

1 ripe pear, peeled, quartered and cored

100 g/⅔ cup chocolate chips (milk or plain)

a large frying pan/skillet or griddle

Serves 4

Begin by preparing the filling. Place the pear quarters in a saucepan or pot of boiling water set over a medium heat and simmer for 20–30 minutes, until the pears are soft. Drain the pears, discarding the liquid, and set aside to cool. Chop the pear into small pieces once cool and mix with the chocolate chips.

Using a sharp knife, cut a pocket in the top of each brioche slice to create a large cavity. Take care not to cut all the way through as it is this cavity which will hold your filling. Spoon a quarter of the filling into each slice and press the opening down to close the pocket.

Whisk together the eggs, cream and caster/granulated sugar in a mixing bowl, transfer to a shallow dish and set aside. Melt the butter in a large frying pan/skillet set over a medium heat until the butter begins to foam. Soak each filled slice in the egg mixture on one side for a few seconds, then turn over and soak the other side. The slices should be fully coated in egg, but not too soggy – it is best to soak one slice at a time. Put each slice straight into the pan before soaking the next slice.

Cook for 2 minutes until the underside of the brioche is golden brown. Sprinkle the top, uncooked side with a little caster/granulated sugar. Add a little extra butter to the pan and turn over and cook for a few minutes further until golden brown. Keep the cooked toast warm while you cook the remaining slices in the same way, adding a little butter to the pan each time, if required.

Serve immediately, dusted with icing/confectioners' sugar, with crème fraîche on the side and any leftover pear, glazed under the grill/broiler and placed on top.

pecan pie french toast

These toasts are inspired by the classic pecan pie – with a crunchy nut coating and a buttery toffee sauce to pour over.

2 eggs

80 ml/scant ⅓ cup double/heavy cream

1 teaspoon ground cinnamon

1 tablespoon caster/granulated sugar

1 teaspoon vanilla extract/vanilla bean paste

140 g/¾ cup pecan nuts, finely chopped

1–2 tablespoons butter, for frying

4 slices white bread

FOR THE SAUCE

40 g/scant ¼ cup caster/granulated sugar

40 g/scant ¼ cup muscovado sugar

1 teaspoon ground cinnamon

1 teaspoon vanilla extract/vanilla bean paste

2 tablespoons butter

2 tablespoons golden syrup/light corn syrup

60 ml/¼ cup double/heavy cream

a large frying pan/skillet or griddle

Serves 4

Begin by preparing the sauce. Put the caster/granulated and muscovado sugar, cinnamon, vanilla extract/vanilla bean paste, butter and golden syrup/light corn syrup in a saucepan or pot set over a medium heat. Simmer until the sugar has dissolved, then add the cream and whisk. Heat for a few minutes longer. Keep the pan on the heat but turn it down to low to keep the sauce warm until you are ready to serve.

For the French toast, whisk together the eggs, cream, cinnamon, sugar and vanilla extract/vanilla bean paste until the mixture is smooth. Place the egg mixture in a wide, shallow dish and the chopped pecans on a plate. Melt the butter in a large frying pan/skillet set over a medium heat until the butter begins to foam. Soak each slice in the egg mixture on one side for a few seconds, then turn over and soak the other side. The slices should be fully coated in egg, but not too soggy – it is best to soak one slice at a time. Carefully move the bread to the pecan plate and coat in pecan crumbs on both sides. Put each slice straight in the pan before soaking and cooking the next slice.

Cook for a few minutes on each side until the slices are golden brown, but taking care that the nuts do not burn. Keep the cooked toast warm while you cook the remaining slices in the same way, adding a little butter to the pan each time, if required.

Serve the toasts with the warm sauce.

peanut butter and jelly french toast

Peanut butter and jelly is a classic American combination. Those of you unfamiliar with it may find the thought of this a little strange but trust me, the sweet and salty combination is delicious and certainly not as peculiar as it sounds. These French toasts are coated in sweet honey-roasted peanuts, but if you like salty flavours you could replace them with crushed salted peanuts instead.

4 large thick slices of brioche or white bread

120 g/1 cup honey roasted peanuts

4 eggs

120 ml/scant ½ cup double/heavy cream

1 tablespoon caster/granulated sugar

a pinch of salt

1–2 tablespoons butter, for greasing

icing/confectioners' sugar for dusting

FOR THE FILLING

3 tablespoons crunchy peanut butter

3 tablespoons fruit jam/jelly (flavour of your choosing)

a large frying pan/skillet or griddle

Serves 4

Using a sharp knife, cut a pocket in the top of each brioche slice to create a large cavity. Take care not to cut all the way through as it is this cavity which will hold your filling. Carefully spread some peanut butter and jam/jelly inside each pocket using a knife, then press the opening down to close the pocket.

Put the peanuts in a food processor and pulse to a fine crumb, then tip onto a large plate and set aside.

Whisk together the eggs, cream, caster/granulated sugar and salt in a mixing bowl, transfer to a shallow dish and set aside. Melt the butter in a large frying pan/skillet set over a medium heat until the butter begins to foam. Soak each filled slice in the egg mixture on one side for a few seconds, then turn over and soak the other side. The slices should be fully coated in egg, but not too soggy – it is best to soak one slice at a time. Carefully move the slices to the peanut plate and coat in fine crumbs on both sides. Put each slice straight in the pan before soaking and cooking the next slice.

Cook for a few minutes on each side until the slices are golden brown, but taking care that the nuts do not burn. Keep the cooked toast warm while you cook the remaining slices in the same way, adding a little butter to the pan each time, if required.

Serve the toasts immediately, dusted with icing/confectioners' sugar.

banana choc chip french toast

Baked bananas, where you wrap bananas in foil with chocolate and cook until the banana is soft and gooey, are a fantastic barbecue dessert. They are the inspiration for this dish. Warm banana and melted chocolate with a crunchy banana crust make these a great breakfast dish that needs no accompaniment.

1 ripe banana, peeled and sliced

freshly squeezed juice of ½ a lemon

50 g/⅓ cup milk/semi-sweet chocolate chips

100 g/1⅓ cups dried banana chips

4 thick slices of white bread or brioche

2 eggs

80 ml/scant ⅓ cup double/heavy cream

1 tablespoon caster/granulated sugar

1 teaspoon ground cinnamon

1–2 tablespoons butter, for frying

icing/confectioners' sugar, to dust

a large frying pan/skillet or griddle

Serves 4

Begin by preparing the filling. In a mixing bowl, mash the banana with the lemon juice to a smooth purée with a fork. Stir in the chocolate chips and set aside.

Blitz the banana chips to fine crumbs in a food processor. Tip onto a plate and set aside.

Using a sharp knife, cut a pocket in the top of each brioche slice to create a large cavity. Take care not to cut all the way through as it is this cavity which will hold your filling. Spoon some of the filling into each slice and press the opening down to close the pocket.

Whisk together the eggs, cream, caster/granulated sugar and cinnamon in a mixing bowl, transfer to a shallow dish and set aside. Melt the butter in a large frying pan/skillet set over a medium heat until the butter begins to foam. Soak each filled slice in the egg mixture on one side for a few seconds, then turn over and soak the other side. The slices should be fully coated in egg, but not too soggy – it is best to soak one slice at a time. Carefully move bread to the banana chip plate and coat in fine crumbs on both sides. Put each slice straight in the pan before soaking and cooking the next slice.

Cook for a few minutes on each side until the bread is golden brown, but taking care that the banana chips do not burn. Keep the cooked toast warm while you cook the remaining slices in the same way, adding a little butter to the pan each time, if required.

Cut the slices into quarters, dust with icing/confectioners' sugar and serve.

chocolate french toast with jaffa cake ice cream

This recipe is dedicated to my friend Jon Lane who loves Jaffa Cakes and is always telling me to write a Jaffa Cake cook book! These French toasts are filled with a delicate layer of marmalade and chocolate chunks, drizzled with chocolate and topped with a wicked Jaffa Cake ice cream. If you cannot find Jaffa Cakes, replace them with chopped orange chocolate instead.

16 slices white bread

2–3 tablespoons fine-shred marmalade/orange jelly

80 g/½ cup milk chocolate, broken into pieces

4 eggs

1 tablespoon cocoa powder, sifted

80 ml/scant ⅓ cup milk

1 tablespoon caster/granulated sugar

1–2 tablespoons butter, for greasing

50 g/½ cup dark/bittersweet chocolate, melted, to drizzle

FOR THE ICE CREAM

400 ml/1⅔ cups double/heavy cream

200 ml/¾ cup milk

100 g/⅔ cup dark/bittersweet orange chocolate, chopped

5 egg yolks

100 g/½ cup caster/granulated sugar

5 Jaffa Cakes or 100 g/⅔ cup orange chocolate, cut into small pieces

a large frying pan/skillet or griddle

9-cm/3½-in circular cookie cutter

an ice cream machine (optional, see Note on page 74)

Serves 4

Begin by making the ice cream. Put the double/heavy cream and milk in a saucepan or pot set over a high heat and bring to the boil. Stir in the orange chocolate until it is melted. This will not take very long. In a mixing bowl, whisk together the egg yolks and caster/granulated sugar until very thick and pale yellow in colour. Pour the hot chocolate milk over the eggs in a thin stream, whisking all the time. Return the mixture to the pan and cook for a few minutes longer, until it begins to thicken. Leave to cool completely. Then churn in an ice cream machine following the instructions on page 74 or the manufacturer's instructions. Once the ice cream is almost frozen, but still soft enough to stir, stir in the Jaffa Cake pieces. Transfer to a freezer-proof container and store in the freezer until you are ready to serve.

For the French toast, cut out 16 circles of bread using the cutter. Discard the crusts. Spread a thin layer of marmalade/orange jelly over the centre of half of the circles and add a few chocolate pieces. Top with a second circle of bread and press down to seal the filling into each sandwich.

Whisk together the eggs, cocoa powder, milk and sugar in a mixing bowl, transfer to a shallow dish and set aside. Melt the butter in a large frying pan/skillet set over a medium heat until the butter begins to foam. Soak each sandwich in the egg mixture on one side for a few seconds, then turn over and soak the other side. The sandwiches should be fully coated in egg, but not too soggy – it is best to soak one slice at a time. Put each slice straight in the pan before soaking and cooking the next slice.

Cook for 2–3 minutes on each side until the egg is cooked and the chocolate chips have melted inside. Keep the cooked toast warm while you cook the remaining slices in the same way, adding a little butter to the pan each time, if required.

Serve each portion drizzled with a little melted chocolate and topped with 2 scoops of ice cream.

nectarine and mascarpone stuffed french toast

The pockets in these French toasts are filled with delicious nectarine and creamy mascarpone cheese. Served dusted with icing/confectioners' sugar and with extra fruit on the side, they are ideal for a brunch gathering with friends. Why not serve a peach bellini cocktail alongside as the perfect accompaniment?

4 thick slices of brioche

2 eggs

80 ml/scant ⅓ cup double/heavy cream

1 tablespoon caster/granulated sugar

1–2 tablespoons butter, for frying

icing/confectioners' sugar, to serve

FOR THE FILLING

the seeds of ½ vanilla pod/bean

125 g/scant 1 cup mascarpone cheese

1 ripe nectarine or peach, stone/pit removed, diced

a large frying pan/skillet or griddle

Serves 4

Begin by preparing the filling. Stir the vanilla seeds into the mascarpone cheese in a mixing bowl, then add the diced nectarine.

Using a sharp knife, cut a pocket in the top of each brioche slice to create a large cavity. Take care not to cut all the way through as it is this cavity which will hold your filling. Spoon a quarter of the nectarine mixture into each slice and press the opening down to close the pocket.

Whisk together the eggs, cream and caster/granulated sugar in a mixing bowl, transfer to a shallow dish and set aside. Melt the butter in a large frying pan/skillet set over a medium heat until the butter begins to foam. Soak each sandwich in the egg mixture on one side for a few seconds, then turn over and soak the other side. The sandwiches should be fully coated in egg, but not too soggy – it is best to soak one slice at a time. Put each sandwich straight in the pan before soaking and cooking the next sandwich.

Cook for 2–3 minutes on each side until the sandwiches are golden brown and the egg is cooked. Keep the cooked toast warm while you cook the remaining slices in the same way, adding a little butter to the pan each time, if required.

Cut the sandwiches in half, dust with icing/confectioners' sugar and serve immediately.

white chocolate macadamia and blueberry stuffed french toast

These toasts have a nutty crust and are bursting with blueberries and melted white chocolate. They are rich and delicious and need nothing more than a light dusting of icing/confectioners' sugar to serve. This is my breakfast of choice to serve to very special friends and family.

4 large thick slices of crusty white bread

4 eggs

120 ml/½ cup double/heavy cream

2 tablespoons caster/granulated sugar

1–2 tablespoons butter, for frying

icing/confectioners' sugar, to dust

FOR THE FILLING

100 g/¾ cup macadamia nuts

60 g/½ cup blueberries

100 g/⅔ cup white chocolate chunks

a large frying pan/skillet or griddle

Serves 4

Begin by preparing the filling. Put the macadamia nuts in a food processor and pulse to fine crumbs. Set aside three quarters of the nut crumb on a plate for the crust and mix the remaining nuts with the blueberries and white chocolate chunks.

Using a sharp knife, cut a pocket in the top of each slice of white bread to create a large cavity. Take care not to cut all the way through as it is this cavity which will hold your filling. Spoon a quarter of the blueberry chocolate mixture into each slice and press the opening down to close the pocket.

Whisk together the eggs, cream and caster/granulated sugar in a mixing bowl, transfer to a shallow dish and set aside. Melt the butter in a large frying pan/skillet set over a medium heat until the butter begins to foam. Soak each sandwich in the egg mixture on one side for a few seconds, then turn over and soak the other side. The sandwiches should be fully coated in egg, but not too soggy – it is best to soak one slice at a time. Carefully move the bread to the nut crumb plate and coat on both sides. Put each sandwich straight in the pan before soaking and cooking the next.

Cook for 2–3 minutes on each side until the egg is cooked and the nut crust is golden brown. Keep the cooked toast warm while you cook the remaining slices in the same way, adding a little butter to the pan each time, if required.

Serve immediately, dusted with icing/confectioners' sugar.

savoury dishes

buttermilk pancakes with salmon and horseradish cream

Bellini pancakes topped with smoked salmon make fantastic canapés. For a more indulgent version why not serve large, fluffy buttermilk pancakes seasoned with chives and topped with thick slices of smoked salmon and horseradish cream? This is great as a brunch dish or a light lunch or supper.

170 g/1⅓ cups self-raising/rising flour, sifted

1 teaspoon baking powder

2 eggs, separated

200 ml/⅔ cup buttermilk

2 teaspoon caster/granulated sugar

1 tablespoon finely chopped chives, plus extra for sprinkling

100 ml/⅓ cup milk

250 ml/1 cup crème fraîche

1 heaped tablespoon creamed horseradish

1–2 tablespoons butter, for frying

400 g/2½ cups smoked salmon, to serve

1 lemon, sliced into wedges

sea salt and freshly ground black pepper, to taste

a large frying pan/skillet or griddle

Serves 4

To make the pancake batter, put the flour, baking powder, egg yolks, buttermilk, caster/granulated sugar and chives in a large mixing bowl and whisk together. Season well with salt and pepper, then gradually add the milk until the batter is smooth and pourable.

In a separate bowl, whisk the egg whites to stiff peaks. Gently fold the whisked egg whites into the batter mixture using a spatula. Cover and put in the refrigerator to rest for 30 minutes.

For the horseradish cream, whisk together the crème fraîche and horseradish in a mixing bowl and season with salt and pepper.

When you are ready to serve, remove the batter mixture from the refrigerator and stir once. Put a little butter in a large frying pan/skillet set over a medium heat. Allow the butter to melt and coat the base of the pan, then ladle small amounts of the rested batter into the pan, leaving a little space between each. Cook until the underside of each pancake is golden brown and a few bubbles start to appear on the top – this will take about 2–3 minutes. Turn the pancake over using a spatula and cook on the other side until golden brown.

Serve the pancakes warm, topped with a generous spoon of the horseradish cream, slices of smoked salmon and wedge of lemon to squeeze over the top. Sprinkle with extra chopped chives and enjoy.

courgette and feta griddle cakes

These pancakes are quick and easy to prepare and make a great accompaniment to soups as an alternative to bread. The feta cheese melts when cooked, giving them a lovely soft texture. I like to make these pancakes with raw courgette, but if you prefer you can fry them until soft in a little olive oil before adding to the pancake batter, making sure that you drain the courgette of its cooking juices and cool first.

150 g/heaped 1 cup self-raising/rising flour, sifted

2 eggs, separated

250 ml/1 cup milk

70 g/4 tablespoons and 1 teaspoon butter, melted and cooled, plus extra for frying

1 teaspoon baking powder

1 large grated courgette/zucchini (approx. 200 g/2½ cups)

200 g/1½ cups feta cheese, crumbled

1 tablespoon freshly chopped mint

sea salt and freshly ground black pepper, to taste

a large frying pan/skillet or griddle

Makes 10

To make the pancake batter, put the flour, egg yolks, milk, melted butter and baking powder in a large mixing bowl and whisk together. Season well with salt and pepper and mix again until you have a smooth batter.

In a separate bowl, whisk the egg whites to stiff peaks. Gently fold the whisked egg whites into the batter mixture using a spatula. Cover and put in the refrigerator to rest for 30 minutes.

When you are ready to serve, remove the batter mixture from the refrigerator and stir gently. Add the grated courgette/zucchini to the batter with the feta cheese and mint.

Put a little butter in a large frying pan/skillet set over a medium heat. Allow the butter to melt and coat the base of the pan, then ladle small amounts of the rested batter into the pan, leaving a little space between each. Cook until the underside of each pancake is golden brown and a few bubbles start to appear on the top – this will take about 2–3 minutes. Turn the pancake over using a spatula and cook on the other side until golden brown. It is important that they cook all the way through to ensure that the middle of your pancakes are not soggy.

Serve immediately.

squash and goat's cheese pancakes

Perfect for lunch, these pancakes are topped with sour cream or crème fraîche and drizzled with delicious pumpkin seed oil. Use a mild, creamy goat's cheese so that the flavour is not overpowering. I love to use Halen Môn sea salt (available online) in this recipe as it is fragranced with cumin, nutmeg, paprika, cloves and cinnamon and goes really well with the spiced squash.

1 butternut squash, peeled and seeds removed (670 g/2½ lb), diced

2 tablespoons olive oil

1 teaspoon black onion seeds

a pinch of spiced sea salt or regular sea salt

4–5 curry leaves, crushed

1–2 garlic cloves, skins on

200 g/1⅔ cups self-raising/rising flour, sifted

2 teaspoons baking powder

1 egg

300 ml/1¼ cups milk

3 tablespoons melted butter, plus extra for greasing

125 g/1 cup soft goat's cheese

sour cream, to serve

a bunch of Greek basil leaves, to garnish

pumpkin seed oil, to drizzle

sea salt and freshly ground black pepper, to taste

an ovenproof roasting pan, greased

a large frying pan/skillet or griddle

Serves 4

Preheat the oven to 180°C (350°F) Gas 4.

Put the diced butternut squash in the prepared roasting pan. Drizzle with the olive oil and sprinkle over the onion seeds, salt and curry leaves. Stir so that the squash is well coated in the oil and spices, then add the garlic cloves to the pan. Roast in the preheated oven for 35–45 minutes until the squash is soft and starts to caramelize at the edges. Leave to cool completely.

To make the pancake batter, put the flour, baking powder, egg and milk in a large mixing bowl and whisk together. Season with salt and pepper. Add the melted butter and whisk again. The batter should have a smooth, dropping consistency. Add about two thirds of the butternut squash to the batter and set aside.

Remove the skins from the garlic cloves and mash to a paste using a fork. Whisk into the batter then crumble in the goat's cheese. Mix together gently. Cover and put in the refrigerator to rest for 30 minutes.

Put a little butter in a large frying pan/skillet set over a medium heat. Allow the butter to melt and coat the base of the pan, then ladle spoonfuls of the rested batter into the pan, leaving a little space between each. Cook until the underside of each pancake is golden brown and a few bubbles start to appear on the top – this will take about 2–3 minutes. Turn the pancake over using a spatula and cook on the other side until golden brown.

Serve the pancakes, topped with a spoonful of sour cream, a few sprigs of basil and the reserved butternut squash. Drizzle with pumpkin seed oil and sprinkle with freshly ground black pepper.

beer and bacon pancakes

These pancakes really are very manly! In place of milk, beer is used to bind the batter. It gives the pancakes a savoury, malty flavour, and with the addition of salty bacon and sweet maple syrup, they really are the perfect sweet and savoury combination.

200 g/1½ cups smoked bacon lardons/diced pancetta

12 slices of smoked streaky bacon/bacon strips, to serve

160 g/1⅓ cups self-raising/rising flour, sifted

1 teaspoon baking powder

1 egg, separated

60 g/⅓ cup dark brown sugar

a pinch of salt

250 ml/1 cup beer (I use Innis and Gunn which has hints of toffee and vanilla)

3 tablespoons melted butter, plus extra for frying

maple syrup, to drizzle

2 large frying pans/skillets or griddle

Serves 6

Begin by frying all of the bacon in a dry frying pan/skillet – they will release sufficient oil as you cook them to prevent them sticking so you do not need to add any extra fat to the pan. Remove from the pan and put on a paper towel to remove any excess fat. Set aside while you prepare the batter.

To make the pancake batter, put the flour, baking powder, egg yolk, dark brown sugar, salt and beer in a large mixing bowl and whisk together. Add in the melted butter and cooked bacon lardons and whisk again. The batter should have a smooth, dropping consistency.

In a separate bowl, whisk the egg white to stiff peaks. Gently fold the whisked egg white into the batter mixture using a spatula. Cover and put in the refrigerator to rest for 30 minutes.

When you are ready to serve, remove your batter mixture from the refrigerator and stir gently. Put a little butter in a large frying pan/skillet set over a medium heat. Allow the butter to melt and coat the base of the pan, then ladle small amounts of the rested batter into the pan, leaving a little space between each. Cook until the underside of each pancake is golden brown and a few bubbles start to appear on the top – this will take about 2–3 minutes. Turn the pancake over using a spatula and cook on the other side until golden brown.

Serve the pancakes with the streaky bacon/bacon strips and lashings of maple syrup.

creamy chicken crêpes

As a child, savoury crêpes really didn't cut it for me! All I wanted was lemon and sugar or maple syrup. As an adult I am a complete convert. The crispy crêpe here acts as a delicious case for the creamy chicken.

140 g/1 cup plain/all-purpose flour

1 egg and 1 egg yolk

2 tablespoons melted butter, cooled, plus extra for frying

300 ml/1¼ cups milk

sea salt and freshly ground black pepper, to taste

FOR THE FILLING

250 ml/1 cup white wine

1 large carrot, peeled and chopped

1 leek, rinsed and sliced

1 onion, peeled and halved

2 bay leaves

1 teaspoon peppercorns

1 medium whole chicken (approx. 1.2-kg/ 2½-lb), rinsed

FOR THE SAUCE

50 g/3½ tablespoons butter

1 onion, peeled and finely chopped

250 g/4 cups chestnut mushrooms, quartered

2 tablespoons cornflour/cornstarch

400 ml/1⅔ cups double/heavy cream

1 tablespoon wholegrain mustard

a large frying pan/skillet, griddle or crêpe pan/machine

a crêpe swizzle stick (optional)

Serves 8

Begin by preparing the filling. Put the wine, carrot, leek, onion halves, bay leaves and peppercorns in a large saucepan or pot and add the whole chicken. Fill the pan with cold water so that the chicken is completely covered. Put the pan over a medium heat and poach the chicken for 1 hour until cooked through. Remove the chicken from the pan. Pass the stock through a sieve/strainer over a bowl, discarding the vegetables, and leave to cool.

Once cool, remove the chicken skin, pull the chicken meat from the bones and cut into bite-sized pieces. Discard the bones and skin. Store the cooked chicken and stock in the refrigerator until needed.

For the sauce, melt the butter in a frying pan/skillet set over a medium heat, then add the onion and cook until translucent and lightly golden brown. Add the mushrooms to the pan and cook for 3–5 minutes until soft. Sift the cornflour into the pan over the mushrooms and stir well. Cook over the heat for a few minutes then add the cream and 200 ml/¾ cup of the reserved chicken stock. Season with salt and pepper and simmer until the sauce thickens. Add the mustard and chilled chicken and stir well to coat everything. Set aside to cool.

To make the crêpe batter, put the flour, egg and egg yolk and melted butter in a large mixing bowl and season with salt and pepper. Whisking all the time, gradually add the milk until you have a smooth and runny batter. Cover and put the batter in the refrigerator to rest for 30 minutes.

When you are ready to serve, remove the batter from the refrigerator and stir gently. Put a little butter in a large frying pan/skillet set over a medium heat. Allow the butter to melt and coat the base of the pan, then ladle some of the rested batter into the pan and quickly spread the batter out very thinly. You can do this either by tilting the pan, or, for best results, use a crêpe swizzle stick. Cook until the top of the pancake is set then turn over carefully with a spatula and cook on the other side for a further 1–2 minutes until the crêpe is golden brown. Keep the crêpes warm while you cook the remaining batter.

Reheat the chicken filling, then spoon it onto one half of each crêpe. Fold the crêpe in half and then half again. Serve immediately with a simple green salad.

gluten-free spinach and ricotta crêpes

These delicate stuffed crêpes are inspired by my friend David Gibbs, who makes the best gluten-free pancakes. The batter is much thinner than traditional crêpe batter. Bright green in colour, these spinach crêpes are filled with ricotta, lemon and parmesan — yum!

80 g/⅔ cup buckwheat flour, sifted

200 ml/1 cup water

2 eggs

1–2 tablespoons butter, for greasing

sea salt and freshly ground black pepper, to taste

FOR THE FILLING

400 g/8 cups spinach, washed and drained

250 g/1 cup ricotta

a pinch of freshly grated nutmeg

freshly squeezed juice of 1 unwaxed lemon plus 1 teaspoon of the grated zest

60 g/scant 1 cup parmesan, plus extra to serve

a large frying pan/skillet, griddle or crêpe pan/machine

a crêpe swizzle stick (optional)

Serves 6

Begin by preparing the filling. Bring a large saucepan or pot of water to the boil over a high heat and season with salt. Add the spinach to the pan and cook in the water for a few minutes until it is just wilted but still vibrant green. Drain and immediately plunge the spinach into cold water. Once cool, put the spinach in a clean tea towel or dish cloth, fold up tightly and squeeze out as much water as possible. Remove a third of the spinach and purée in a food processor with 1 tablespoon of water. Set the purée aside until you are ready to cook the crêpes.

Finely chop the remaining spinach and mix together with the ricotta. Season with salt and pepper, nutmeg and the lemon juice and zest. Fold in the parmesan then store in the refrigerator.

To make the crêpe batter, put the flour, water, eggs and reserved spinach purée into a large mixing bowl. Season with salt and pepper and whisk until you have a smooth and runny batter. Cover and put the batter in the refrigerator to rest for 30 minutes.

When you are ready to serve, remove the batter from the refrigerator and stir gently. Put a little butter in a large frying pan/skillet set over a medium heat. Allow the butter to melt and coat the base of the pan, then ladle a spoonful of the rested batter into the pan and quickly spread the batter out very thinly. You can do this either by tilting the pan, or, for best results, use a crêpe swizzle stick. Cook until the top of the pancake is set then turn over carefully with a spatula and cook on the other side for a further 1–2 minutes until the crêpe is crispy. Keep the crêpes warm while you cook the remaining batter.

Put some of the chilled ricotta filling in the centre of each crêpe and roll up to serve. Top with a little extra grated parmesan if desired.

ham and cheese crêpes

Ham and cheese crêpes are very popular in France. I remember eating them with my host family on a school French exchange programme, many years ago now! They are filled with a delicate béchamel sauce and ham, rolled up and topped with grated cheese which melts when they are baked in the oven.

140 g/1 cup plain/all-purpose flour

1 egg and 1 yolk

2 tablespoons melted butter

2 teaspoons wholegrain mustard

300 ml/1¼ cups milk

120 g/1 cup wafer thin ham

150 g/1½ cups emmental cheese, grated

sea salt and freshly ground black pepper, to taste

FOR THE SAUCE

825 ml/3⅓ cup milk

1 small onion, peeled and kept whole

1 teaspoon black peppercorns

2 bay leaves

a pinch of freshly grated nutmeg

75 g/5 tablespoons butter

75 g/½ cup plain/all-purpose flour, sifted

a large frying pan/skillet, griddle or crêpe pan/machine

a crêpe swizzle stick (optional)

Serves 8

Begin by preparing the béchamel sauce. Put the milk in a saucepan or pot set over a medium heat. Quickly add the onion, peppercorns, bay leaves and nutmeg and bring the milk to the boil. Remove from the heat and leave to infuse for 30 minutes. Strain the sauce through a sieve/strainer over a bowl and discard the onion, leaves and peppercorns. In a separate saucepan or pot set over a medium heat, melt the butter until it starts to foam. Tip in all of the flour in one go, remove the pan from the heat and beat the mixture hard until the flour is incorporated and you have a thick paste which leaves the sides of the pan. Reheat the milk and add a little at a time to the flour paste, beating well over the heat as the milk is added. When all the milk is incorporated you should have a smooth white sauce. Season with salt and pepper to taste. Cover and set aside.

To make the crêpe batter, put the flour, egg and egg yolk, melted butter and mustard in a large mixing bowl. Season well with salt and pepper. Whisking all the time, gradually add the milk until you have a smooth and runny batter. Leave the batter to rest in the refrigerator for 30 minutes.

When you are ready to serve, remove the batter from the refrigerator and stir once. Put a little butter in a large frying pan/skillet set over a medium heat. Allow the butter to melt and coat the base of the pan, then ladle a spoonful of the rested batter into the pan and quickly spread the batter out very thinly. You can do this either by tilting the pan, or, for best results, use a crêpe swizzle stick. Cook until the top of the pancake is set then turn over carefully with a spatula and cook on the other side for a further 1–2 minutes until the crêpe is golden brown. Keep warm while you cook the remaining batter.

Preheat the oven to 190°C (375°F) Gas 5.

Spread a generous spoonful of béchamel over each crêpe and top with a few slices of ham. Sprinkle with a little of the cheese and then roll up the crêpe. Place in the ovenproof dish and repeat with all the remaining crêpes. Pour the rest of the béchamel sauce over the pancakes and sprinkle with the remaining cheese. Bake in the preheated oven for 10–15 minutes until the cheese has melted and turns golden brown. Serve immediately.

potato waffles with barbecue beans

Barbecue beans are among my top comfort foods. They are great as a side dish and remind me of evenings spent open-air camping, with sausages and beans simmering over glowing embers. Served here with delicious potato waffles, this recipe is comfort food heaven.

2 baking potatoes

260 g/2 cups self-raising/rising flour, sifted

1 teaspoon baking powder

a pinch of salt

3 eggs, separated

300 ml/1¼ cups milk

60 g/4 tablespoons butter, melted

a handful of grated cheddar or Emmental cheese, to serve

FOR THE BEANS

1 tablespoon olive oil

1 medium onion, peeled and finely sliced

1–2 garlic cloves, peeled and finely sliced

400 g/2 cups canned chopped tomatoes

2 tablespoons Worcestershire sauce

2 tablespoons soy sauce

40 g/¼ cup dark brown sugar

480 g/3¼ cups cooked cannellini beans, drained and rinsed

sea salt and freshly ground black pepper, to taste

an electric or stove-top waffle iron

a baking sheet lined with baking parchment

Serves 4

Preheat the oven to 200°C (400°F) Gas 6.

Prick the potatoes with a fork and bake them in the preheated oven on the prepared baking sheet for 1 hour–1¼ hours (or in a microwave on full power for about 8 minutes per potato). Leave the potatoes to cool, then cut them open and remove the potato from the skins. Mash the flesh with a fork and discard the skins.

For the beans, heat the olive oil in a large saucepan or pot set over a medium heat. Add the sliced onion and cook until they turn translucent. Add the garlic to the pan and cook for a few minutes longer until the onion and garlic are lightly golden brown. Add the tomatoes to the pan and season well with salt and pepper. Add the Worcestershire sauce, soy sauce and dark brown sugar and simmer until the sauce becomes thick and syrupy. Put the beans in the sauce and simmer for a further 20 minutes. Keep the pan on the heat but turn it down to low to keep the beans warm until you are ready to serve.

In a large mixing bowl, whisk together the cooled mashed potato, flour, baking powder, salt, egg yolks, milk and melted butter until you have a smooth batter. In a separate bowl, whisk the egg white to stiff peaks. Gently fold the whisked egg whites into the batter mixture using a spatula.

Preheat the waffle iron and grease with a little butter.

Ladle some of the batter into the preheated waffle iron and cook for 3–5 minutes until golden brown. Keep the waffles warm while you cook the remaining batter.

Serve the waffles topped with the hot barbecue beans and grated cheese.

ginger and sesame waffles with steak and dipping sauce

Steak and dipping sauce is a classic. These steaks are served with delicious sesame waffles to help mop up the juices.

3-cm/2-in piece of ginger, peeled

260 g/2 cups self-raising/rising flour, sifted

1 teaspoon baking powder

a pinch of salt

3 eggs, separated

375 ml/1½ cups milk

75 g/5 tablespoons butter, melted, plus extra for greasing

2 tablespoons finely chopped fresh coriander/cilantro

1 tablespoon sesame seeds

2–4 beef fillet steaks

sea salt and freshly ground black pepper, to taste

a bunch of fresh coriander/cilantro, to garnish

FOR THE SAUCE

80 ml/scant ⅓ cup tamari soy sauce

60 ml/¼ cup Worcestershire sauce

60 ml/¼ cup maple syrup

1 heaped tablespoon tomato ketchup

1 tablespoon olive oil

1 tablespoon sesame seeds

1 tablespoon freshly chopped coriander/cilantro

freshly ground black pepper, to taste

an electric or stove-top waffle iron

a large frying pan/skillet or griddle

Serves 4

To make the waffle batter, purée the ginger in a food processor, adding a little water if necessary. In a large mixing bowl, whisk together the flour, baking powder, salt, egg yolks, milk and melted butter until you have a smooth batter. Add the ginger purée, coriander/cilantro and sesame seeds and whisk again.

In a separate bowl, whisk the egg whites to stiff peaks. Gently fold the whisked egg whites into the batter mixture using a spatula.

Preheat the waffle iron and grease with a little butter.

Ladle some of the batter into the preheated waffle iron and cook for 2–3 minutes until golden brown. Keep the waffles warm while you cook the remaining batter and are ready to serve.

For the dipping sauce, put all of the ingredients in a bowl and whisk together well.

Season the steaks with salt and pepper and sear in a frying pan/skillet set over a high heat. The cooking time will depend on how rare you like your meat. Sear for about 1–2 minutes on each side for rare and 3–4 minutes each side for well done, depending on the thickness of your steaks.

Slice the steaks very thinly and serve on top of 2 waffles per person with fresh coriander/cilantro and the dipping sauce on the side.

huevos rancheros

Huevos Rancheros or 'ranch eggs' are a traditional Mexican breakfast of spicy tomatoes with eggs served on corn tortillas. This version uses corn waffles in place of the tortillas. Although the tomatoes are traditionally cooked, I prefer tomato and avocado salsa as the taste is much fresher. Wake up your senses with a kick of piquant paprika and the delicate fragrance of coriander.

160 g/1⅓ cups self-raising/rising flour, sifted

100 g/1 cup fine yellow cornflour/cornstarch

1 teaspoon bicarbonate of soda/baking soda

1 tablespoon caster/granulated sugar

3 eggs, separated

375 ml/1½ cups milk

60 g/5 tablespoons butter, melted

1 tablespoon olive or vegetable oil

8 eggs

70 g/scant 1 cup cheddar cheese, grated

sour cream, to serve

sea salt and freshly ground black pepper, to taste

FOR THE SALSA

4 large tomatoes, halved

2 ripe avocados

freshly squeezed juice of 2 limes

2 heaped tablespoons finely chopped fresh coriander/cilantro

½ teaspoon hot paprika, plus extra for sprinkling

an electric or stove-top waffle iron

a large frying pan/skillet or griddle

Serves 4

To make the waffle batter, put the flour, cornflour, bicarbonate of soda, caster/granulated sugar, egg yolks, milk and melted butter in a large mixing bowl. Whisk until you have a smooth batter. Season with salt and pepper. In a separate mixing bowl, whisk the egg whites to stiff peaks and then gently fold into the batter a third at a time.

Preheat the waffle iron and grease with a little butter.

Ladle some of the batter into the preheated waffle iron and cook for 2–3 minutes until golden brown. Keep the waffles warm while you cook the remaining batter and are ready to serve.

For the salsa, remove the seeds from the halved tomatoes using a teaspoon and discard. Cut the hollowed out tomatoes into small pieces using a sharp knife. Prepare the avocado by removing the stones and skins and cutting the flesh into small pieces. Immediately mix the avocado with the lime juice and tomatoes so that it does not discolour. Add the coriander/cilantro, sprinkle over the paprika and stir in. Season with salt and pepper and set aside in the refrigerator until needed.

Heat the oil in a frying pan/skillet and fry the 4 eggs for 2–3 minutes until the whites of the eggs are cooked but the yolks are still soft and runny.

Place the waffles on plates and top with a generous portion of the salsa. Place the fried eggs on top and sprinkle over the grated cheese. Top with a spoonful of sour cream and a pinch of paprika, and serve straight away.

welsh rarebit waffles

Welsh rarebit is so simple to prepare and makes a lovely supper, whether topping toast, a crumpet or, as in this recipe, a savoury waffle. Melted cheese with mustard and tangy Worcestershire sauce served with roasted vine tomatoes and a crisp green salad — what could be better?

200 g/1⅔ cups self-raising/rising flour, sifted

3 eggs, separated

250 ml/1 cup milk

70 g/5 tablespoons butter, melted

sea salt and freshly ground black pepper, to taste

FOR THE ROASTED TOMATOES

300 g/1⅓ cups vine cherry tomatoes

1–2 tablespoons olive oil

1 tablespoon balsamic glaze

1 tablespoon caster/granulated sugar

FOR THE TOPPING

300 g/3½ cups cheddar cheese, grated

1 egg

2 teaspoons wholegrain mustard

1 tablespoon Worcestershire sauce, plus extra to splash

an electric or stove-top waffle iron

Serves 6

Begin by preparing the tomatoes. Preheat the oven to 180°C (350°F) Gas 4. Put the tomatoes in the roasting pan and drizzle with olive oil, the balsamic glaze and caster/granulated sugar. Season with salt and pepper and roast in the preheated oven for 20–30 minutes until the tomatoes are soft and their juices start to run. Keep warm until you are ready to serve.

To make the waffle batter, put the flour, egg yolks, milk and melted butter into a large mixing bowl. Whisk until you have a smooth batter. Season with salt and pepper. In a separate mixing bowl, whisk the egg whites to stiff peaks and then gently fold into the batter a third at a time.

Preheat the waffle iron and grease with a little butter.

Ladle some of the batter into the preheated waffle iron and cook for 2–3 minutes until golden brown. Keep warm while you cook the remaining batter and are ready to serve.

For the topping, put all the ingredients into a bowl and mix.

Spread a large spoonful of the cheese mixture over each waffle and place under a hot grill for a few minutes until the cheese melts and starts to turn golden brown. Watch carefully to make sure that the rarebit topping and waffle do not burn, turning the grill/broiler heat down if required. Splash the tops of the waffles with a few drops of Worcestershire sauce and serve immediately with the roasted tomatoes on the side.

spicy french toast

The egg mixture used here is flavoured with delicious spices and hints of chilli, garlic and ginger. Served with a coriander and coconut chutney they make a great brunch or supper dish. You can use any type of bread; I prefer sourdough as it has a tangy taste which compliments the spices in the dish.

2 teaspoons cumin seeds

a bunch of fresh coriander/cilantro leaves, plus extra to garnish

2½-cm/1-in piece of ginger, peeled

1 large garlic clove

1 red chilli, stalk and seeds removed

1 teaspoon garam masala

1 tablespoon melted ghee or butter, plus extra for frying

4 eggs

2 tablespoons milk

a pinch of salt

8 slices sourdough bread

FOR THE CHUTNEY

320 ml/1¼ cups coconut milk

1 red chilli, stalk and seeds removed

1 tablespoon tamari soy sauce

1 tablespoon Thai fish sauce

1 tablespoon caster/granulated sugar

freshly ground black pepper

2½-cm/1-in piece of ginger peeled and chopped

1 garlic clove

a large frying pan/skillet or griddle

Serves 4

Begin by making the chutney. Put all of the ingredients in a food processor and blend for 15–20 seconds. Scrape down the sides of the food processor and blend again for a few more seconds until the chutney is completely smooth. Chill in the refrigerator before serving.

In a dry frying pan/skillet set over a medium heat, toast the cumin seeds for a few minutes until they start to pop. Take care that they do not burn. Set aside to cool.

Blend together the coriander/cilantro, ginger, garlic, chilli, garam masala and melted ghee or butter in a food processor until you have a smooth paste. Transfer the paste to a large mixing bowl and whisk together with the eggs, milk, salt and toasted cumin seeds.

Melt a little butter or ghee in a large frying pan/skillet set over a medium heat until the butter begins to foam. Soak each slice of bread in the spiced egg mixture on one side for a few seconds, then turn over and soak the other side. The slices should be fully coated in the egg mixture, but not too soggy – it is best to soak one slice at a time.

Cook for 2–3 minutes on each side until the egg is cooked and the slices are lightly golden brown on both sides. Keep the spicy breads warm until you have cooked all the slices. Put each slice straight in the pan before soaking and cooking the next slice.

Serve immediately with the chutney and garnish with torn fresh coriander/cilantro.

french toast with asparagus and hollandaise

Hollandaise sauce and asparagus are one of life's sweetest luxuries. The key is to cook the hollandaise very slowly and add the butter gradually, to prevent the velvety sauce from splitting. It is most commonly flavoured with lemon, but in this version I use orange and basil vinegar in the reduction instead. If you do not have basil vinegar, you can add 2–3 basil leaves to the reduction or just replace it with white wine or sherry vinegar.

14–16 asparagus spears, trimmed

3 eggs

4 slices of white bread

sea salt and freshly ground black and pink pepper, to taste

FOR THE SAUCE

80 ml/scant ⅓ cup basil vinegar or white wine vinegar

1 shallot, finely chopped

1 teaspoon black peppercorns

the grated zest of 1 unwaxed orange

3 egg yolks

175 g/1 stick plus 3 tablespoons butter, melted, plus extra for frying

a large frying pan/skillet or griddle

Serves 2

Begin by making the hollandaise sauce. Put the vinegar, chopped shallot, peppercorns and orange zest in a saucepan or pot set over a medium heat and simmer until the mixture reduces and becomes syrupy – you should be left with 1–2 tablespoons of liquid. Remove from the heat and strain through a sieve/strainer over a bowl to remove and discard the zest, peppercorns and shallots. Put the bowl over a pan of simmering water on a very low heat and add the egg yolks. Whisk until the mixture is very thick, then add the melted butter 1 spoonful at a time, whisking continuously. The important thing is to keep the heat very gentle so that the eggs do not overcook. If the sauce splits, then add 1 tablespoon of ice cold water or an ice cube and whisk well to re-emulsify the sauce.

While the hollandaise is cooking, put the asparagus in a steaming basket over a pan of boiling water, sprinkle with a little sea salt, and steam for about 3–4 minutes until it is soft but still has bite.

For the French toast, beat the eggs in a mixing bowl and season well with salt and pepper. Melt the butter in a large frying pan/skillet set over a medium heat until the butter begins to foam. Soak each slice in the beaten egg mixture on one side for a few seconds, then turn over and soak the other side. The slices should be fully coated in egg, but not too soggy – it is best to soak one slice at a time. Put each slice straight in the pan before soaking and cooking the next slice.

Cook for 2–3 minutes on each side until the egg is cooked and the slices are lightly golden brown. Keep the toasts warm while you cook the remaining slices.

Serve two slices of French toast per portion topped with asparagus and a generous spoonful of the hollandaise sauce.

tricolore french toast

This savoury French toast is delicious and filled with the flavour of Italy — mozzarella, basil and sundried tomatoes. Serve with spicy tomato chutney or green salad on the side, or even wrapped up for a picnic lunch.

4 thick slices of bread

150–200 g/1–1½ cups mozzarella, thinly sliced

12 sun blushed tomatoes

a handful of basil leaves, chopped

2 eggs

60 ml/¼ cup milk

1–2 tablespoons butter, for frying

sea salt and freshly ground black pepper, to taste

a large frying pan/skillet or griddle

Serves 4

Using a sharp knife, cut a pocket in the top of each slice of bread to create a large cavity. Take care not to cut all the way through as it is this cavity which will hold your filling. Stuff each slice with the mozzarella, tomatoes and a little of the basil. Press the opening down to close the pocket.

Whisk together the egg and milk in a large mixing bowl and season with salt and pepper, then whisk in the remaining basil. Melt the butter in a large frying pan/skillet set over a medium heat until the butter begins to foam. Soak each sandwich in the beaten egg mixture on one side for a few seconds, then turn over and soak the other side. The slices should be fully coated in egg, but not too soggy – it is best to soak one slice at a time. Put each sandwich straight in the pan before soaking and cooking the next toast.

Cook for 2–3 minutes on each side until the egg is cooked and the slices are lightly golden brown and the cheese has melted. Keep the toasts warm while you cook the remaining sandwiches.

Serve immediately.

index

acknowledgments

Very many thanks to Ryland Peters & Small for allowing me
to spend many days cooking my favourite pancakes and waffles –
in particular to my special friend Julia Charles for commissioning the
book, Stephanie Milner for her patient editing and Lauren Wright for the
wonderful PR support. To Steve Painter for his stunning design and
photography – you are quite literally a genius! Love and thanks to Lucy
McKelvie and Ellie Jarvis for the beautiful food styling! Heartfelt thanks to
my agent Heather Holden-Brown, Claire and Elly for their unending support.
To my brother Gareth, Amy and Hunter, for all the New York French toast
inspiration – I love you guys. To my Mum and Dad for always being there,
to Josh and Rosie, my "tastebuds", who critiqued nearly all the recipes in this
book and to my friends Lucy, David, Jess, Miles, Maren, Justina, Debs, Jon,
Rachel, Alison, Darren, Ella, Torin, Kathy, Simon, Podington Sewing Circle,
Millie, Andrew, Zara, Laren, Mike, Liz, Jane, Geoff, Fay, Tom, Luke, Steve,
Mags, Shivaji, Ishan and Kiran – thank you for eating all the pancakes,
waffles and French toasts!